D0895141

# All About Radio and Television

# All About Radio and Television

By Jack Gould

*Radio and Television Editor, The New York Times*

*Illustrated by* Bette J. Davis

RANDOM HOUSE
NEW YORK

To Carmen

SECOND EDITION

TWELFTH PRINTING

 Published in New York by Random House, Inc., and simultaneously in Toronto, Canada, by Random House of Canada, Limited.

MANUFACTURED IN THE U.S.A.

LIBRARY OF CONGRESS CATALOG CARD NUMBER: *58-9449*

# Acknowledgment

I wish to express my indebtedness to the American Radio Relay League, national organization of amateur radio operators, for its assistance in the preparation of this book.

George Grammer, Technical Editor of "QST," the league's monthly publication, and John Huntoon, assistant secretary of the league, gave most generously of their time to read the manuscript and offer many valuable suggestions.

JACK GOULD

*Old Greenwich*
*Connecticut*

# Table of Contents

# 1.

# Television is Fun

Flick on the switch of your television set. The big screen lights up, and the whole world marches into your living room.

Maybe it is a funny man telling a joke that makes you laugh. Maybe it is a ballplayer hitting a home run in the World Series. Maybe it is the President of the United States making a speech.

Whatever it is, you know the program is taking place miles away—in a theater, in a major league baseball park or in the White House in Washington.

But right in your own home you see and hear everything that happens. So do millions and millions of other people all the way from Maine to California and from Canada to Texas.

Television is indeed wonderful. Yet for all its wonder we know that operating a television set is easy.

First you turn the dial to get the program you want. Twirl a knob, and you can make the picture brighter or darker. Turn another knob and you can make the sound just right—not too loud and not too soft. That's all there is to it.

What we cannot see are the strange and fascinating things that happen inside a set when we turn these knobs.

The way a television program is sent through the air into your home may seem like magic. It is magic if you don't know how television works. If you do know, it is very simple.

In fact, how television works is so simple that you yourself can have fun doing some of the tricks that it took scientists years and years to discover. Many of the tricks have been used for a long time in radio to send sound through the air. All television does is take these old tricks and use them in a new way to send pictures through the air.

# 2.

# Making a Wave

To learn about television we must do something you may have done many times before. We must stand by a pond and throw a rock into the water.

When the rock hits the water, it makes a big splash. Then we see waves going out in big circles like this:

Let's see what makes these waves. When you threw the rock into the pond, it took energy. It was the energy in your arm and body that made the rock go through the air and into the water.

When the rock hit the pond, it disturbed the water. As the rock went down, the only place the water could go was up like this:

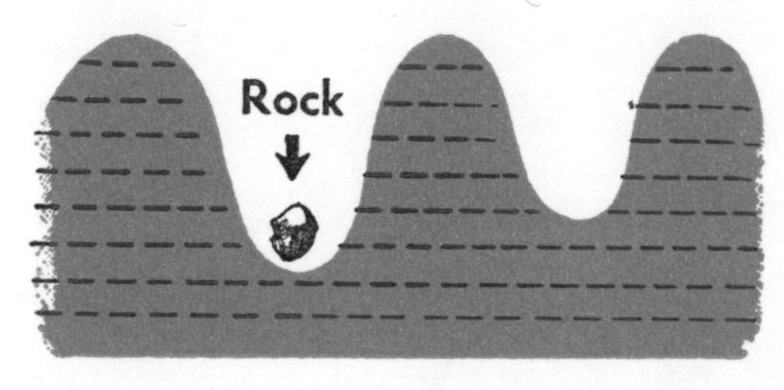


What goes up must come down, so this ring of water came down and pushed away more water. This happened over and over again, and in a moment or two we saw the circles of waves stretch out across the pond.

We know the waves made by the rock are pretty to watch, but let's see how they are useful too.

Take a fishing pole and a line. On the end of the line, tie a cork. Just let the cork float on top of the water. Now throw another rock into the pond. Out come the waves again in big circles.

But look at the cork. It bobs up and down when it is hit by the waves.

What made the cork bob? It wasn't the rock, because that fell straight to the bottom of the pond. No, the waves made the cork bob.

But what makes the waves? Energy makes the waves. So what do the waves carry between the place where the rock falls in and where the cork floats? That's right: *energy*. As a matter of fact, we can call it a wave of energy because that's exactly what it is.

There's another way to show how energy can travel in a wave.

Take a piece of string and tie it to a doorknob. Now hold the other end of the string in your hand and give it a shake. It looks like this:

When you shake the string, a wave of energy travels along the string up to the doorknob.

But whether we make waves of energy by throwing rocks into a pond or shaking a rope tied to a door, we do know one thing is the same. We only make the waves when we disturb the water or the rope. If the water and the rope are not moving, then we cannot have waves.

Now let's think about another kind of wave that we use all the time but cannot see. It is the sound wave. Every time you talk you make a sound wave. What happens is this: your voice disturbs the air around your mouth just like the rock disturbed the water in the pond.

Hold the palm of your hand just as close to your mouth as you can. Make sure it doesn't touch your lips. Now say "Hello" in a loud voice.

You can feel a wave of air like your breath pushing against the palm of your hand.

Now say "Hello" softly. You can feel a little wave of air pushing against your hand.

These waves of air are made by the energy you use in speaking. They travel out into the air much as the waves of water traveled across the pond.

The reason we can hear these waves as sound is because your ear acts like the cork tied to the fishing line. Inside your ear is a tiny drum. You know that with a real drum you can make a sound by beating the drum with a stick.

Inside your ear it is the wave of air carrying a sound that strikes your eardrum. A big wave of sound gives the eardrum a big push, just as a big wave of water gives the cork a big push. A little wave of sound gives the eardrum a little push. The pushes that the drum receives are then sent up to your brain which turns them into sounds that you recognize.

So far we have talked about waves of energy that we can either hear or see. We could not do without these waves, but both kinds have something the matter with them. The trouble with these waves is that they cannot travel very far.

If you are too far away, you cannot hear another person and you cannot see him.

But we are lucky. There is another kind of wave of energy that can travel as far as we want it to go. This is a wave made by electricity. You cannot see this wave of energy with just your eye or hear it with just your ear, but it is there all the same.

There is, however, something else we can do. We can use special equipment to change one kind of wave into another kind of wave. We can take waves that we can see or hear and turn them into waves of electricity. Or we can take waves of electricity and change them back into sight and sound waves.

This is what we do in television. We start with one kind of a wave, turn it into another kind, and then change it back again.

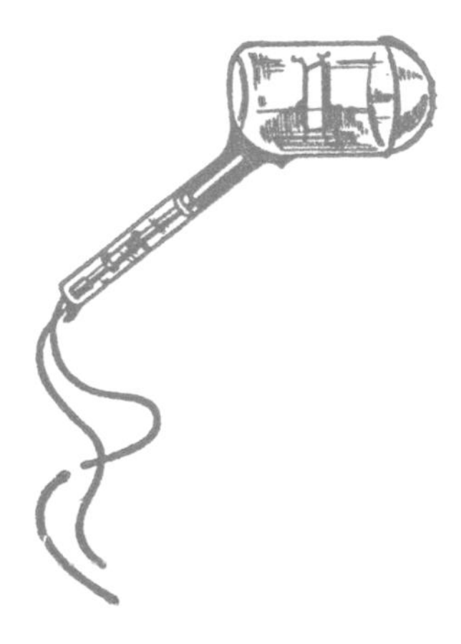

# 3.

# Making a Television Wave

A wave of energy made by electricity often seems mysterious because you can neither hear nor see it. But there is another way to learn about this wave; we can find out what it can do. That's almost as good.

You have seen a toy magnet made in the shape of a horseshoe. And you know what happens when you bring it near a tack like this:

The tack jumps to the magnet like this:

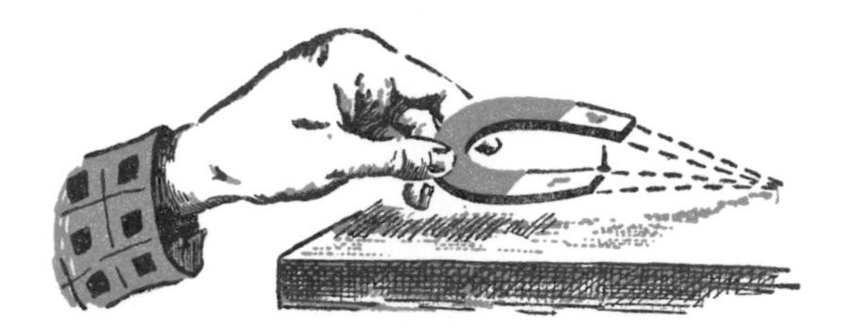

But what made the tack jump? There was nothing you could see; there was nothing you could touch.

It was an invisible force sent out by the magnet that made the tack move. This force is one of the wonders of nature. It was first discovered thousands of years ago and is called *magnetism.* Without magnetism we could not have electric lights, the telephone, the telegraph, radio or television.

There is another easy experiment to try with a magnet. Bring a compass near a magnet, and you will see the needle spin around like this:

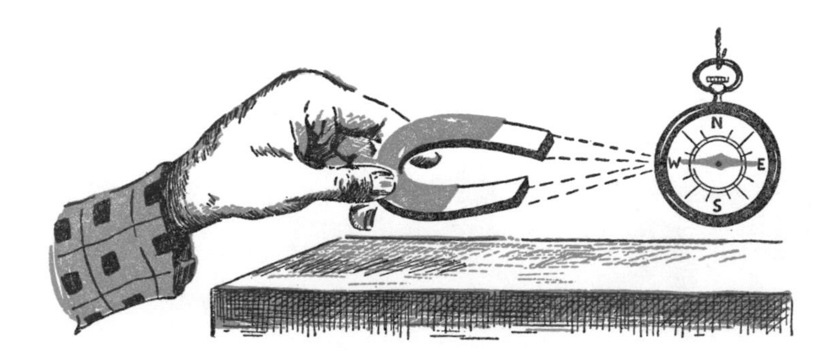

The force of the magnet makes the needle turn.

Let's try something else. Let's see if there is another way to make a compass needle move.

Here is a wire. From a battery we will send a current of electricity around the wire like this:

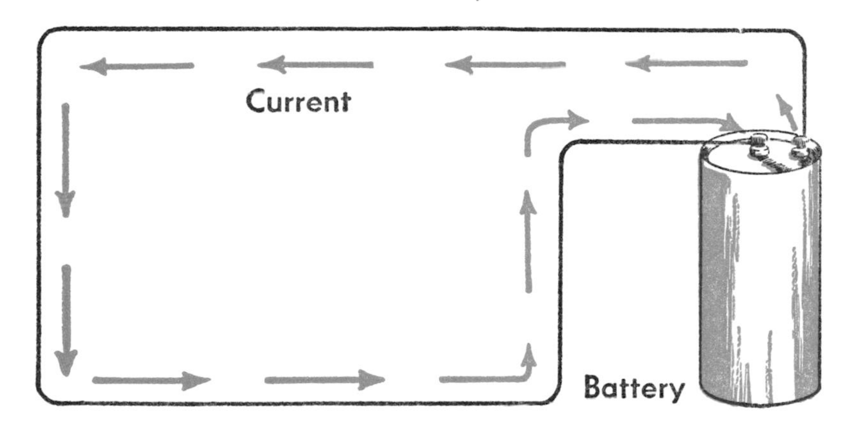


Bring the compass near the wire through which the electricity is passing.

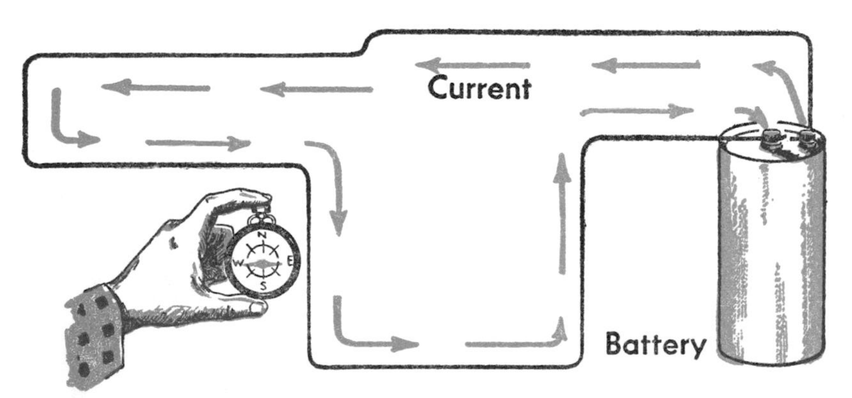


The needle spins around toward the wire!

Can you guess what caused the needle to spin? It was a force of magnetism. You can prove this easily. Disconnect the wire from the battery, and see what happens. The needle goes back to its original place.

In other words, electricity going through a wire acts like a magnet. It is a very weak magnet. But there is an easy way to make a strong magnet with electricity.

We can make a strong magnet by putting a lot of wire into a small space. To do this, we wind the wire into a coil. Let's hook up the coil to the battery, like this:

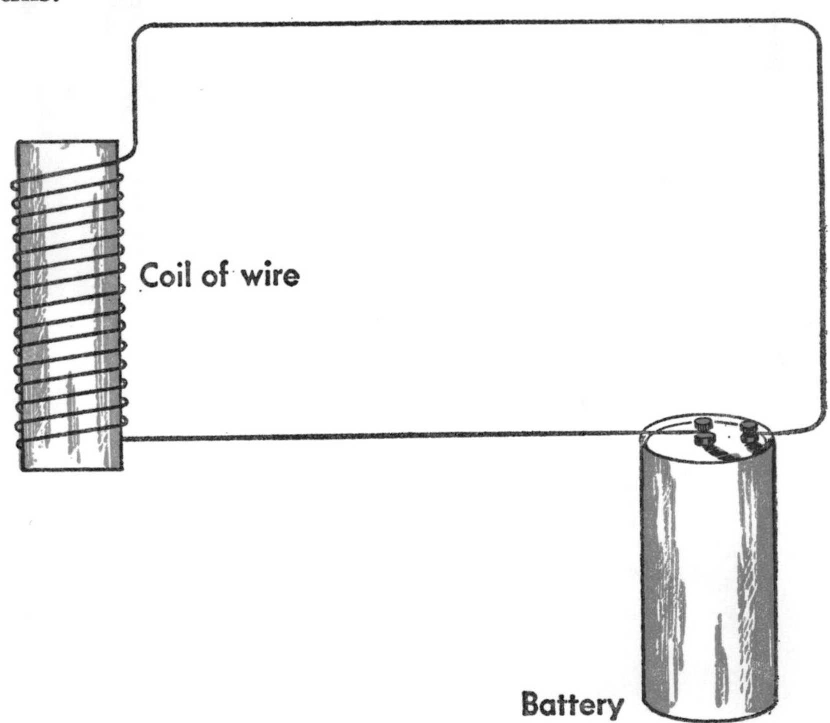

When we send a current of electricity through the coil now, it makes a big force of magnetism which we can show like this:

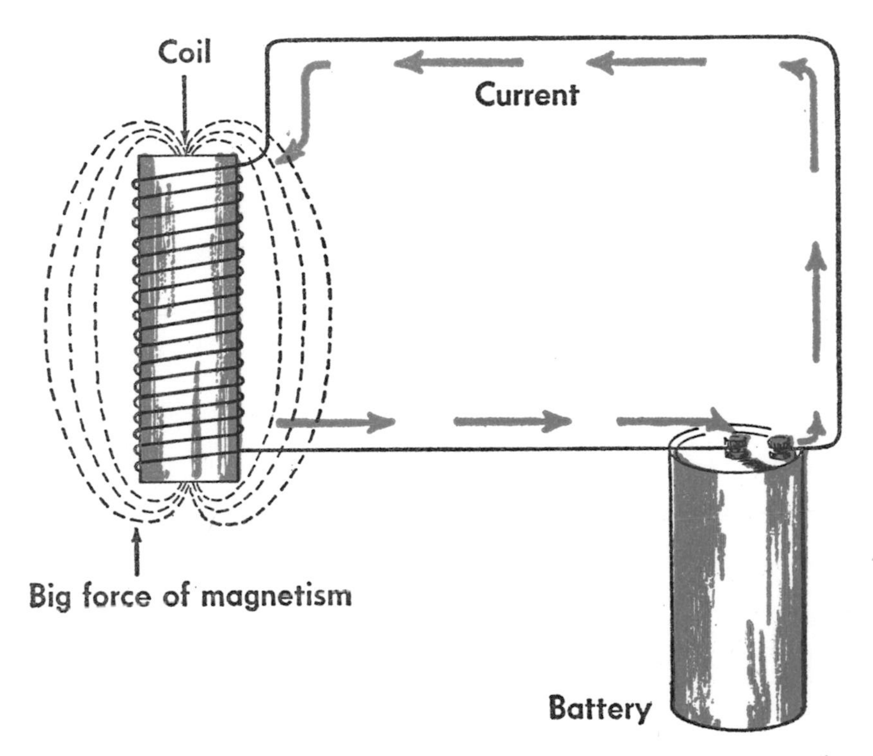


You can see that this big force of magnetism looks like our old friend—the waves of water in the pond. In fact, it really is a wave of energy. And because it takes both electricity and magnetism to make this kind of wave, scientists call it an *electromagnetic wave.*

But a wave of energy made by electricity is also like the wave of water in another respect. After a while it will just die out unless we find a way to keep making new waves.

Every time we wanted to send electricity through the coil we could hook up the battery, disconnect it after the electricity had gone through the coil, and then hook it up again. But that would be an awful nuisance. There is a much easier way.

We can use a generator that sends electricity first in one direction and then in another. When electricity goes first one way and then another, it is called an *alternating current* because its direction is always changing. When the electricity only goes in one direction, it is called a *direct current.*

Hook up the coil to the generator and now send the current of electricity back and forth:

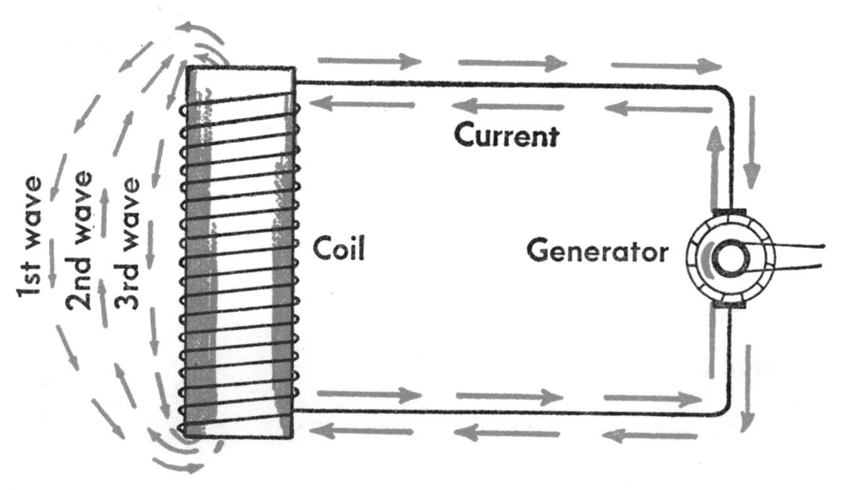

See what's happened to the first wave made by the electricity. It has been pushed away from the coil by the second wave. And the second wave has been pushed away by the third. This goes on and on until the waves go farther and farther away.

Because the waves are made by electricity going first one way and then another, we can show them by arrows pointing in opposite directions.

But it is not necessary to send the waves away from the coil itself. We can hook a wire to the coil and then run the wire up to the top of a tall tower. When we do this, the waves are sent out from the tower in big circles like this:

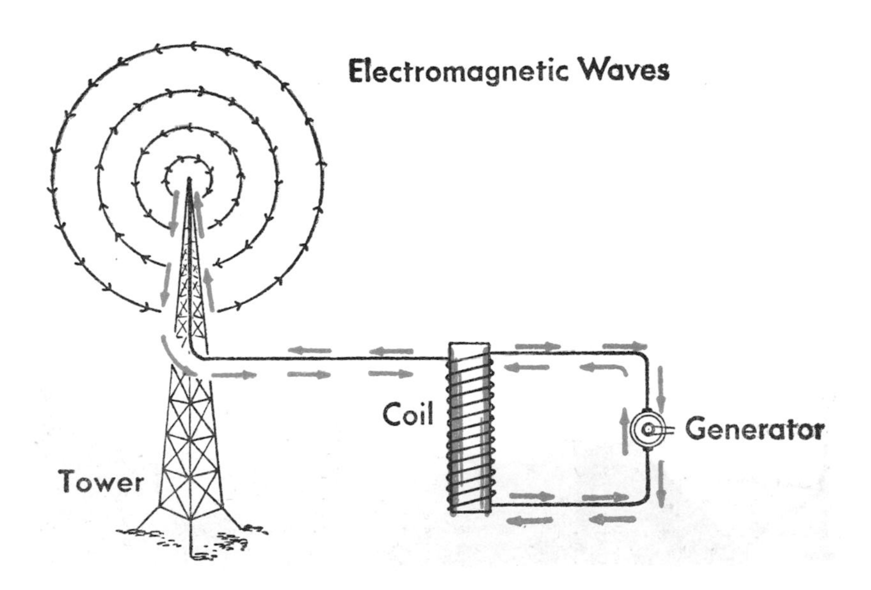

The equipment that sends out waves is called a *transmitter*. The word transmit means to send along.

If these electromagnetic waves just stay in space, they will not be of any use and will disappear. But they do something wonderful if they come to another wire or metal rod miles away from the broadcasting station.

You remember how the waves of water gave the cork a little push to make it bob and the waves of sound gave a push to the drum in your ear. The electromagnetic waves behave in much the same way.

When these waves come to a rod, they make a current of electricity move back and forth in the rod like this:

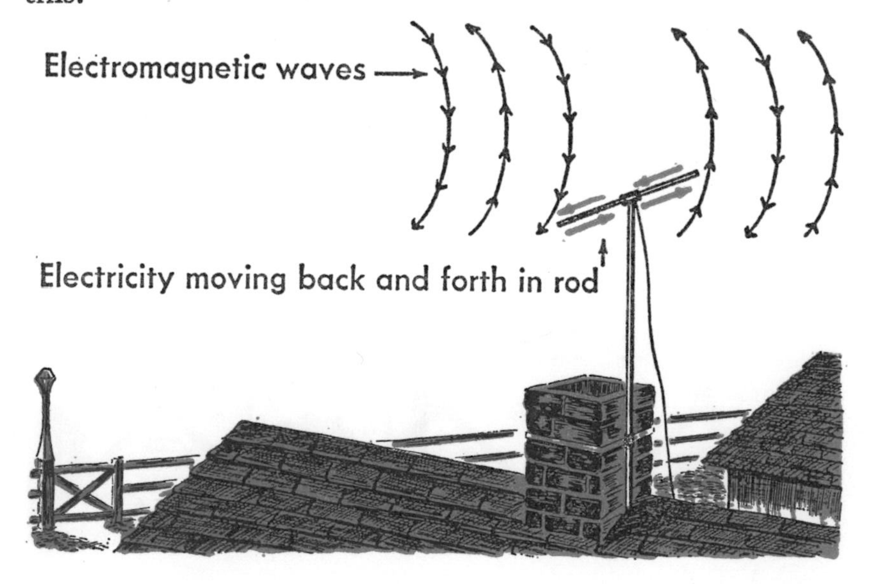

We used a wire to connect the coil to the top of the transmitter tower. In the same way we can connect one end of a wire to a rod on top of a house and the other end to a television set downstairs in the living room. With this wire we lead the current of electricity made by the waves right into the set.

It does not make any difference how many rods we put up to catch the waves. Electricity will be made in each rod when the rod is crossed by the waves.

Now you can understand why millions of people can receive a television program. Each family just puts up its own rod—called an *aerial;* and its own wire connecting the rod to the set—called a *lead-in wire.*

This is how several houses would look, if we could see the electromagnetic waves and the electricity they made:

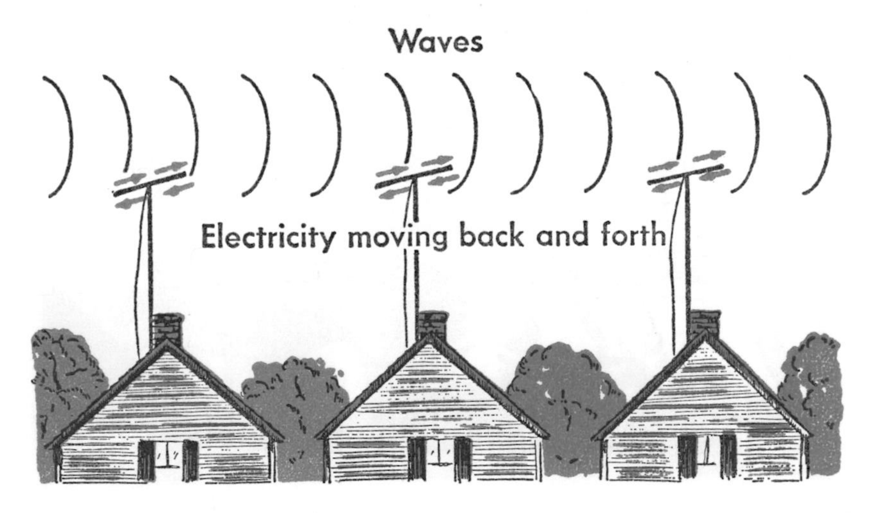

But there's something especially remarkable about these waves. That's the speed with which they move.

Say out loud this word: *ONE.*

In the time that it took you to say *ONE*, can you guess how far an electromagnetic wave traveled? The wave traveled 186,000 miles. That is more than seven times around the world.

Because the waves move so fast and go out in all directions, millions of families can see and hear the same thing at the same time.

# 4.

# Changing a Picture Into Electricity

In television we know we have a current of electricity moving back and forth at the transmitter. And we have a current of electricity moving back and forth at the receiver.

Let's see now how these two movements of electricity can be compared to a boy and girl riding a bicycle built for two like this:

No matter how many times the boy pedals around with his feet, the girl must pedal around the same number of times. The chain on the bicycle links the pedals together, and the feet of the boy and the feet of the girl move up and down together.

The television transmitter and the television receiver act in much the same way as the feet of the boy and girl.

No matter how many times the electricity goes back and forth through the coil at the transmitter, we can be sure the electricity in the aerial wire goes back and forth the same number of times. The electromagnetic waves are a sort of invisible chain between the two.

In fact, this invisible link is the secret of sending pictures and sounds through the air. We can make any changes we want in the electricity at the broadcasting station, and we know the same changes will be made in the electricity in the aerial wire that is connected to the set.

This is the first step in broadcasting. We make something happen at a station, and we can be sure that the same thing will happen in all the places where there is a receiver.

## Changing a Picture Into Electricity

So what we must do now is take a picture and a sound and turn them into changes of electricity. Does that seem hard? It isn't.

Let's take the picture first. You know that we must have a camera in the studio. But you may not know that a television camera does not take the whole picture at once like the box camera that you may have used at home. A television camera takes a picture in lots of little pieces, and then the pieces are put back together on the screen in your home.

See if you can find a magnifying glass. Hold the magnifying glass over a picture in a newspaper. Look carefully, and you will see hundreds and hundreds of little black and white dots. Actually, a picture is made with dots, but they are so small you see only the complete picture. But if we can put dots together to make a picture, we can also take them apart. In television that's what we do.

The camera focuses on a scene in a studio. Then it makes a change of electricity for each black and white dot in the picture.

You can think of the camera as an electrical "gate." Into the camera from one side comes a flow of electricity always going in the same direction. Out the other side is a wire to carry whatever electricity the camera lets through. This is the way that would look:

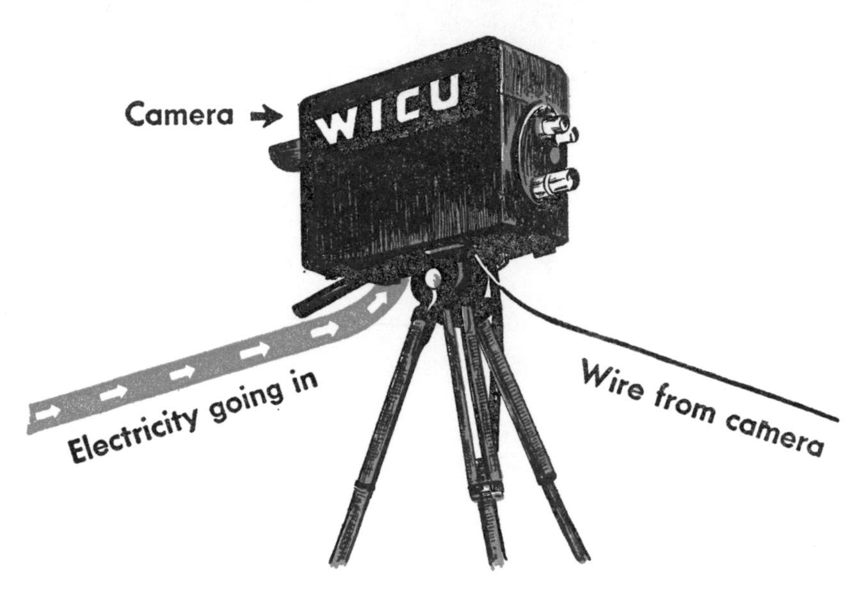


Turn on the camera, and let's see what happens. Remember we know that a picture is made up of black dots and white dots.

The camera picks up a black dot. At that instant the camera lets through a big burst of electricity. Then the camera picks up a white dot. At that instant it lets through a little burst of electricity.

What do we have now? We have first a big burst of electricity for the black dot and a little burst for the white dot. We can show these changes in the electricity like this:

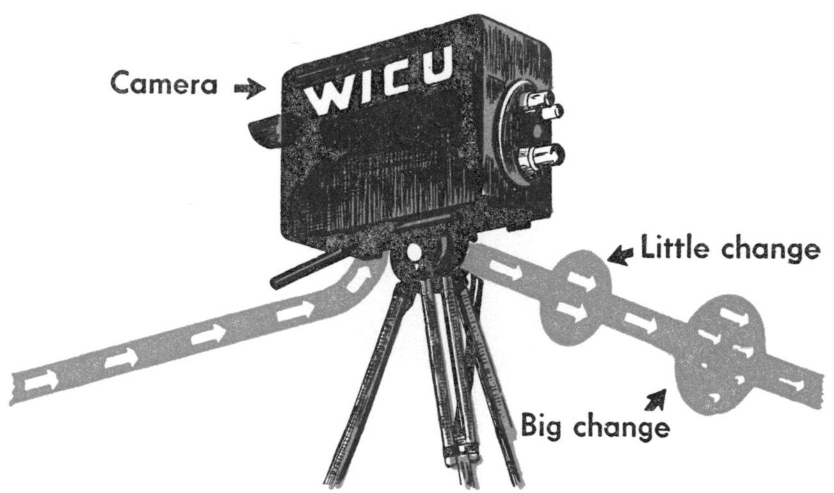


All the camera must do is catch all the black and white dots in a picture and turn the whole picture into bursts, or changes, of electricity. Later you will learn about the inside of a camera and understand how this is done.

Now let's turn sound into bursts, or changes, of electricity. For this we use a microphone, and it behaves very much like the camera. It also is a "gate," which lets through the big and little bursts of electricity.

Remember how your voice made a big push of air against your hand when you spoke loudly? And a little push when you spoke softly?

Just as we divided a picture into black and white dots, we can think of sounds as loud and soft.

This time, imagine you say a loud HI and a soft *ho*. When the loud HI is picked up, the microphone lets through a big burst of electricity. When the soft *ho* is picked up, the microphone lets through a little burst of electricity.

The inside of a microphone works very simply so we can explain it right away.

You will remember that when you speak you disturb the air around your mouth and send out big and little waves of air that carry the sound.

Inside the microphone is a very thin plate of metal. Behind the metal are tiny little bits of carbon. This is the way the microphone looks:

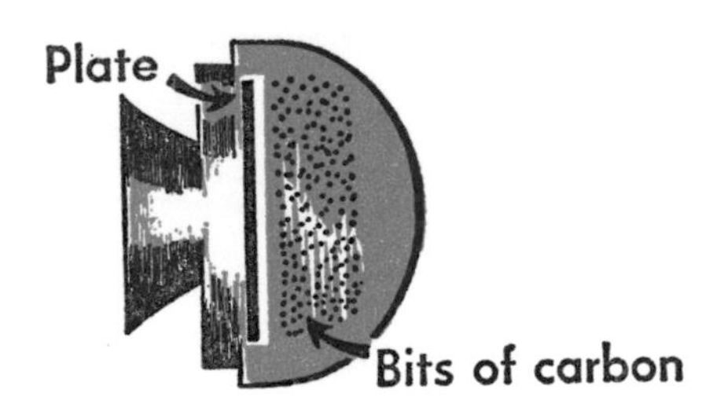


When you say a loud HI, you make a big sound wave that pushes up against the plate just as it pushed up against the palm of your hand. The plate, in turn, pushes all the bits of carbon close together.

When the carbons are all squeezed together, they are like a nicely paved sidewalk. Then it's easy for the electricity to rush through.

When you say a soft *ho*, you only make a small sound wave. It doesn't push the plate so hard and doesn't squeeze all the bits of carbon together so closely. Then the bits of carbon look more like a rock walk, and it's much harder for the electricity to get through the microphone. This is how the electricity must go:

You can see that the loud sound lets a big burst of electricity get through the microphone because it makes a smooth road of carbons. The soft sound only lets a small burst of electricity through because it makes a rough road of carbons.

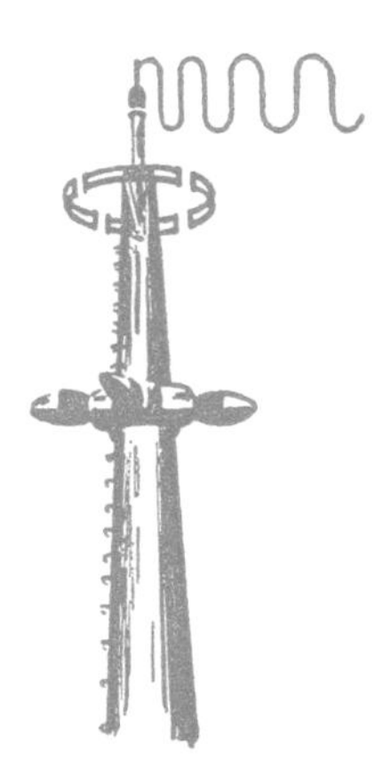

# 5.

# Sending the Waves

The camera and the microphone have done their work. By letting through big and little bursts, they have made the changes in electricity at the broadcasting studio. Now we must see how those changes can be put on the waves that are sent out into space.

First, we know that if we are going to see a picture or hear a sound in our receiver there must be a continuous chain of waves going across the sky between the station and the receiver in the home. If the waves stop, the picture and the sound will stop.

We know the waves are made by electricity that goes back and forth in different directions. So we show the *carrier waves* like this:

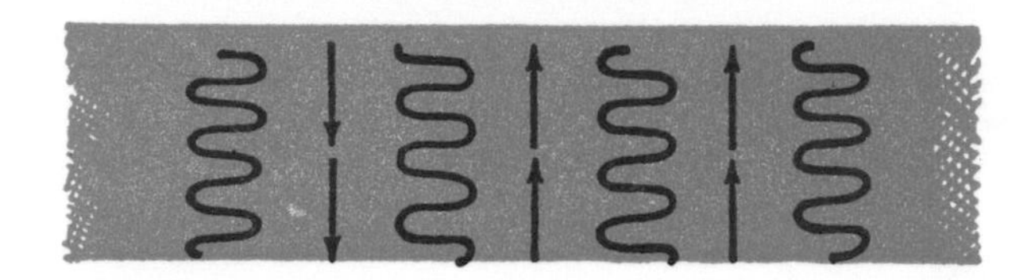

Now let's go back to the rope tied to the door. Suppose we give the rope a big shake like this:

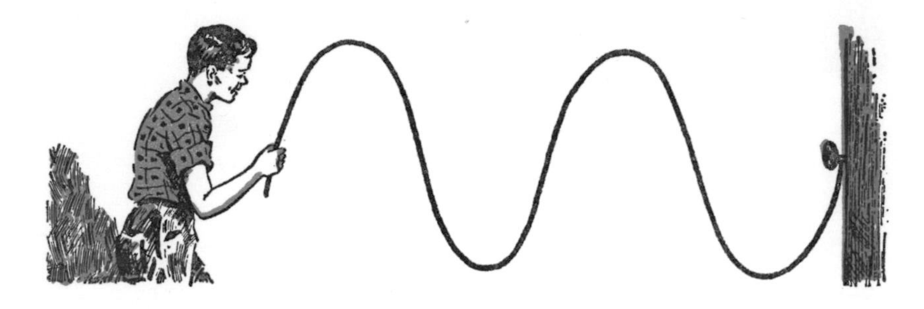

Look at the tops of the waves in the rope. They are very high because you have given the rope a big shake.

Now give the rope a little shake like this:

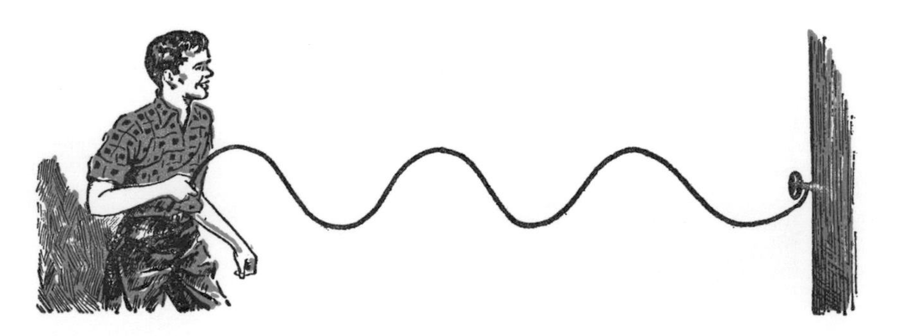

The tops of the waves are much lower.

Now try one more test with the rope. Give it first a big shake and then a little shake. The waves could be shown like this:

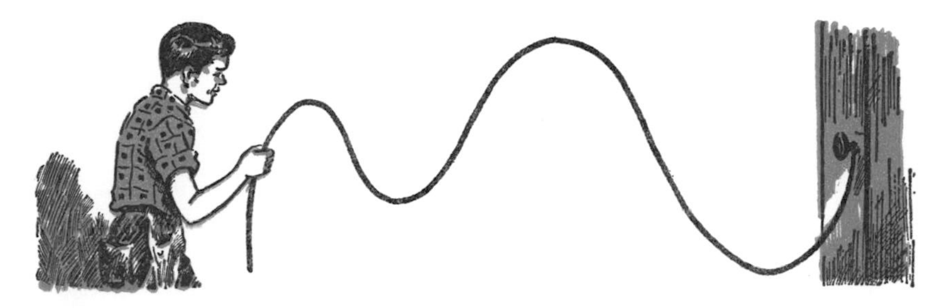

You can see that we can send big and little changes in energy along the rope by making big and little waves.

That's what we do in television. We can send big and little changes in electricity through the sky by making the carrier wave first big and then little.

We do this by mixing the carrier waves and the changes in electricity from the camera or the microphone. Look what happens when they meet:

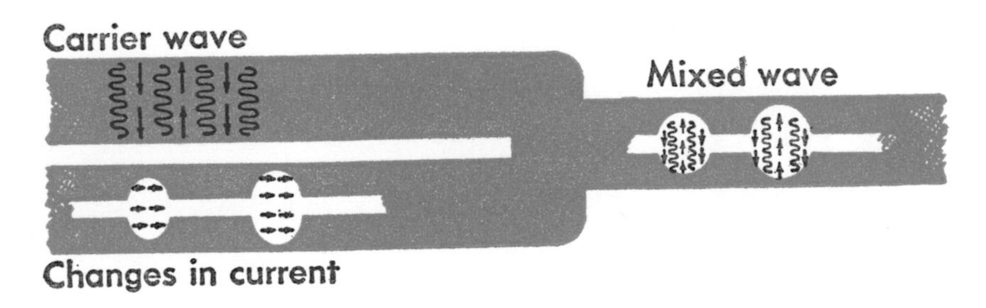

The carrier waves are no longer all the same size. They have been shaped into big and little waves by the big and little changes in electricity. But they still go back and forth in both directions just like the electricity that we used in the coil to make the carrier waves.

This shaping of carrier waves is called *modulating* the waves. Perhaps you have heard of *amplitude modulation*, or AM for short. Amplitude is just a fancy word for strength. In modulating the waves, we have changed their strength. The waves are strong when they carry the black dot from the picture or a loud sound; they are weak when they carry a white dot or a soft sound.

All regular radio stations use AM to send out programs, and television stations use AM to send out pictures.

But there is another way to shape or modulate a wave. Perhaps you have heard of it. It is called FM, which stands for *frequency modulation*. All television stations use FM to send the sound.

With FM we do not change the height of the carrier waves. Instead, we vary the number of waves we make. With a loud sound we make many waves;

with a soft sound, just a few. This is the same as saying we vary the frequency of the wave. First we give the frequency a big wiggle and then a little wiggle. Now, when the waves carry a loud HI and a soft *ho*, we can show them like this:

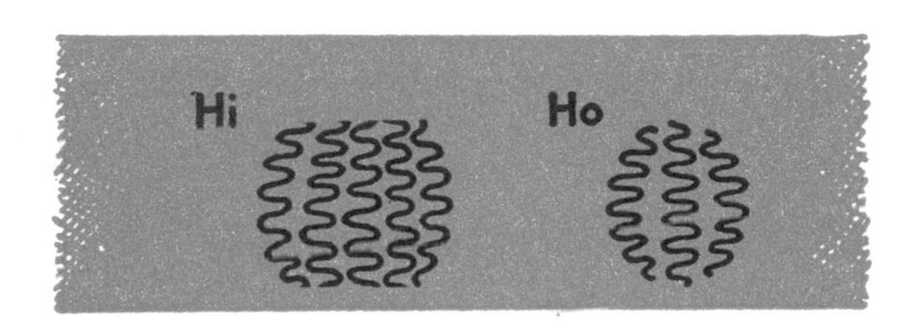


There is a big advantage to FM—it gives clearer reception. Scientists worked long and hard to learn how to send the waves they want, but sometimes they have trouble with waves they do not want. These waves are called *static*. During a thunderstorm you may hear static making a crackling, spluttering noise in the loud-speaker. Or you hear it when somebody runs an elevator or when a refrigerator is turned on.

Lightning and motors act like crazy radio stations. They send out waves that change in height or amplitude. These waves sneak into a radio along with the waves that you want to hear. They are like electrical mosquitoes, buzzing around and making a nuisance of themselves.

But an FM set will let only FM waves get through to the loud-speaker; it turns back the AM waves made by the lightning and motors. So with FM there is no annoying static.

As you can see, a television station is really two stations in one. One station broadcasts the picture and the other the sound. Each shapes its own carrier waves, and these waves go across the sky, side by side like a brother and sister walking down the street. Similarly, a television receiver is really two sets in one. One receives the picture and one the sound.

To tell one part from another scientists use special words. The picture part is called *video*. *Video* is the Latin word meaning "I see." The sound part is called *audio*. *Audio* is the Latin word meaning "I hear."

# 6.

# Receiving the Waves

Once we have shaped our carrier waves, they travel out in all directions from the transmitting tower. Now we are ready to see what happens after these waves have traveled through space and finally come to your home.

You will remember that the waves make electricity go back and forth along the rod which we have put up on the roof. And then we can lead this electricity down to the television set in your living room on a lead-in wire.

Here comes the big wave made by the black dot

in the picture that was picked up by the camera in the broadcasting studio. Right behind it comes the little wave made by the white dot:

When the big wave reaches the aerial, it makes a big burst of electricity move back and forth on the rod and down the wire leading to the television set in the living room. The little wave makes a little burst.

Coming into the set there are really two changes in electricity—a big change and a little change. That's what we want: the same kind of changes in electricity at the receiver as were made by the camera and the microphone at the broadcasting studio.

But do you remember how the changes at the studio looked? They looked like this:

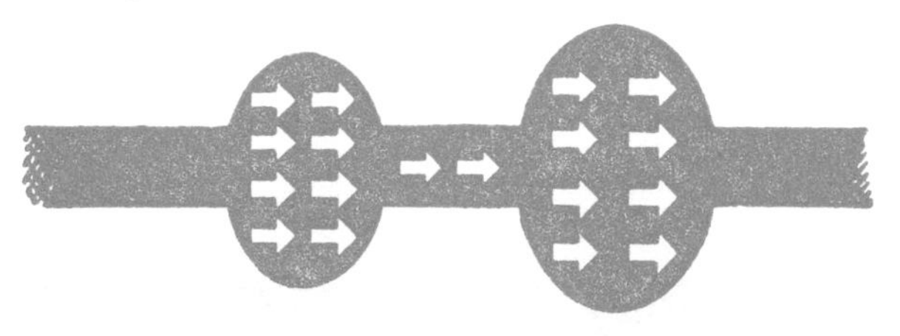

And these are the changes that have come into our receiver:

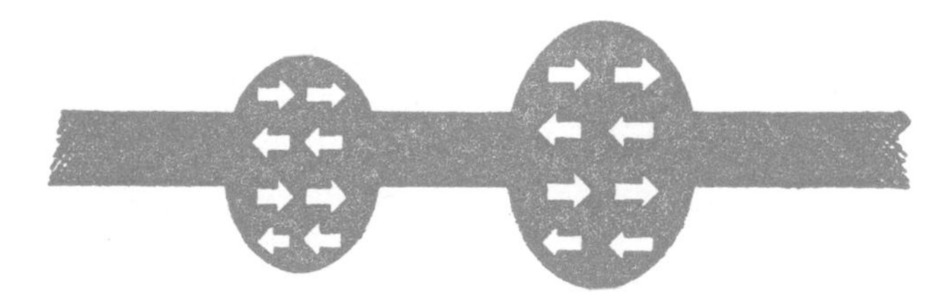

The changes are almost alike, but not quite.

The changes made by the camera and the microphone at the studio show electricity that always moves in the same direction. But the changes made by the waves show electricity that is moving in two directions, first one way and then the other.

You can see now what we must do. We must keep all the current that is moving in one direction and throw away the current that is going in the other direction.

We can do this by a very easy trick. Inside the set

we build a "gate" that will only let current pass in one direction. This "gate" is called a *detector.*

We can show the detector and what it does to the current like this:

Current coming in Current going out

What we have really done is take a current of electricity that moves in both directions—*alternating current*—and turn it into electricity that moves in one direction—*direct current.*

Now here are the changes in electricity made by the big and little waves when they come to the detector:

Changes coming in Changes going out

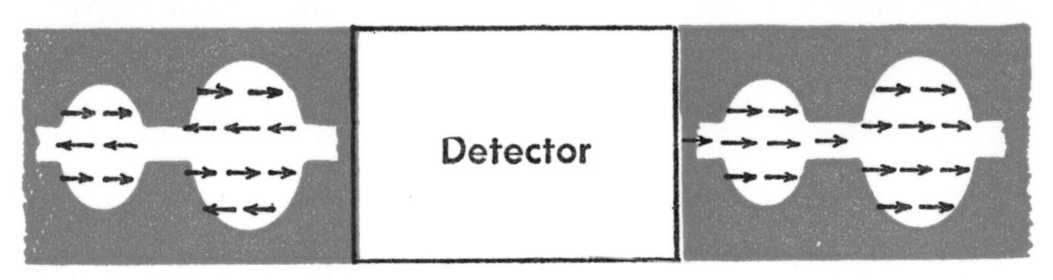


We have just what we want!

We have big and little changes in electricity that are just the same as the big and little changes made by the camera and the microphone. The rest is easy.

The big change in electricity goes to the screen of the receiver and makes a black dot on the screen. Then the little change in electricity comes along and makes a white dot. One after the other come all the big and little changes for all the black and white dots in the picture. When all the black and white dots are in their places on the screen, we see the complete picture.

You have heard the expression that the camera is quicker than the eye. But it may be hard to realize how much quicker television is.

Every second all the dots in the picture reach the screen of your set not once but thirty separate times. That's why you never miss anything and always see a complete picture.

We send sound into the air on the same kind of waves as we send pictures—on AM waves that are either strong or weak. When we do this, we have the same kind of changes of electricity coming into our set. These changes also go to the detector so that the electricity is all going in the same direction.

With FM waves—waves which are the same strength but vary in number—we do something different inside the set. We use a kind of electrical pump.

With a loud sound a lot of waves come close together. Then we have a big wiggle in the frequency. That works the pump hard and sends out a big burst of electricity. When a few waves come together, as with a soft sound, we have a small wiggle that does not work the pump so hard. It makes a little burst of electricity.

But once we have the changes in electricity, whether by AM or FM, we send them to the loud-speaker in the same way. This is how the loud-speaker works:

You remember what happened when we put a magnet near a tack. The tack was pulled to the magnet. And you know that we can make a magnet by sending electricity through a coil of wire.

But there is something further we can do. We can put a bar of metal inside the coil. Then when we send electricity through the coil, the end of the bar also will act like a magnet. Now instead of using a tack, suppose we put a metal disk in front of the bar like this:

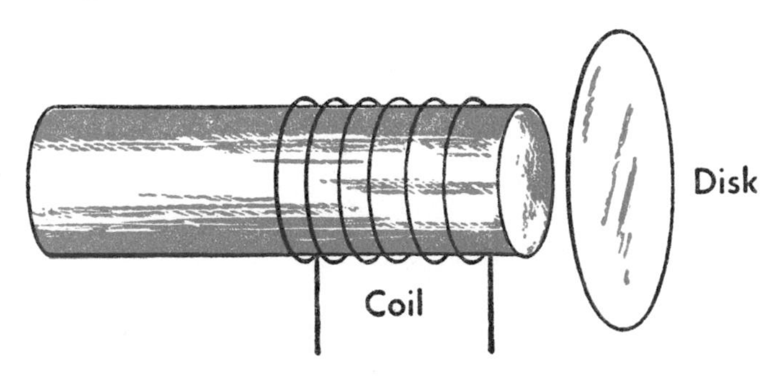

When we send a big burst of electricity through the coil, we make a strong magnet. The metal disk is pulled toward the bar like this:

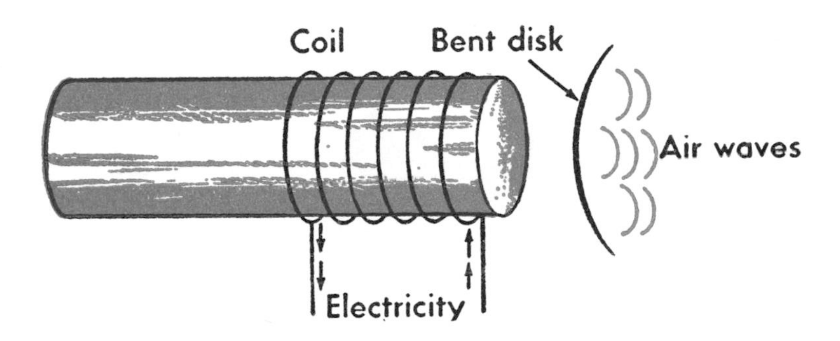


When we send a little burst of electricity through the coil, we make a weaker magnet and the metal disk is pulled only a little way.

When the disk is pulled back, it disturbs the air around the disk. These disturbances make little waves of air that we hear as loud and soft sounds.

Disks are used inside a telephone or in earphones where your ear is close to the coil. But when we want to operate a loud-speaker, we must be able to make much bigger disturbances in the air so that we can hear sounds all over a room.

Perhaps you have been to a football game and have seen the cheer leaders use megaphones so that they can be heard by people sitting in the grandstands.

In a loud-speaker we use a paper cone that works like the megaphone. We connect the cone to the disk like this:

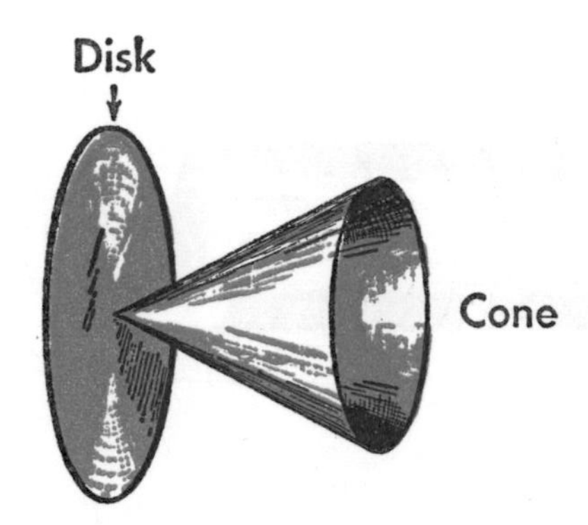


Now send a big burst of electricity through the coil:

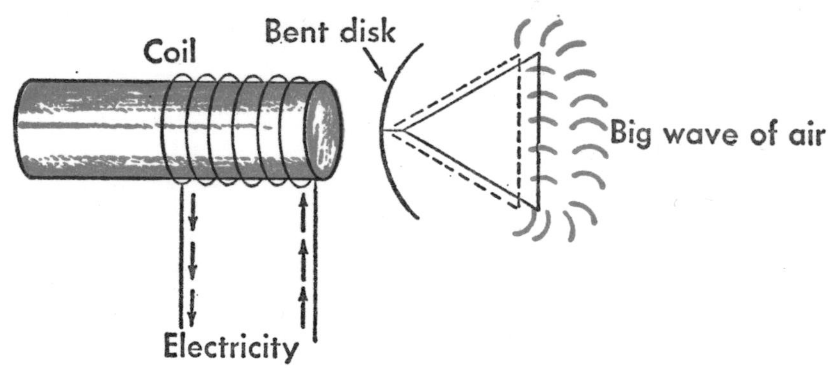


The magnet again pulls the disk, and the disk, in turn, pulls the paper cone. The movement of the cone disturbs the air and this makes big waves of air that you hear as a loud sound.

Put your hand in front of a loud-speaker. You can feel the waves of air. They are just like the waves of air that you felt when you said "Hello" loudly into the palm of your hand.

Now you can see why the sound that comes out of a loud-speaker is always the same as the sound that goes into the microphone. The changes in electricity going through the microphone and the loud-speaker are always the same.

Whether a program going through the air is a picture or a sound, there always is an easy way to remember how it makes the trip from the station to your receiver. It's just like mailing a puzzle to a friend. First, you start with the puzzle all put together. Then, you take the puzzle apart and send the pieces to your friend. Finally, your friend puts the pieces back together again.

# 7.

# Picking the Program You Like

All the members of a family can have a good time watching television, but sometimes they have a problem.

Dad and the boys in the family may want to watch a baseball game, but Mother and Sister may want to see a play. Or, perhaps, the big brother wants to see a movie and the little brother wants to watch a puppet show.

Everybody in the family soon learns there is only one solution to the problem. The television set must be shared so that everyone has a chance to see what he likes.

But think how much worse it would be if there were no way to tune in one program and tune out another. Suppose everything—the baseball game, the play, the movie and the puppet show—all appeared on the same screen at the same time. The screen would look as if it had gone crazy. There would be just jumbled lines, and we could not see any one program clearly.

Luckily there is a way to keep one station separate from another. You know this when you switch to Channel 2 or Channel 4 on a television set. Or when you turn the dial on a radio set to 66 to receive one station or to 88 to receive another.

We can choose one particular station because of an interesting thing about all kinds of waves. Each wave can have a number just as we give each automobile its own number on a license plate. This does not change the wave. It just lets us know how to find the wave when we want it.

The number we give a wave is decided by a very simple method: how often the wave is made. If a wave is made five times in a second, we could call it a No. 5 wave. And if it is made ten times in a second, we could call it a No. 10 wave.

But there is a better way to say the same thing. Let's have another look at the rope tied to the door-knob. This time we will shake the rope so it makes nice smooth waves like this:

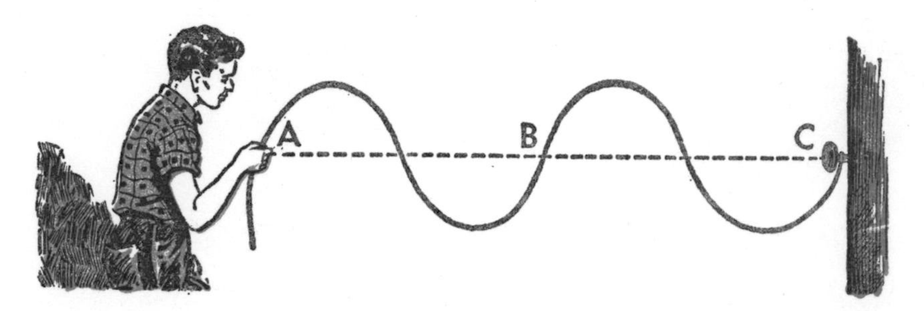


You can see we really have made two waves. The first wave starts at A, goes up and down and finally comes back to the level it started from—at B. The second wave starts at B, goes up, down and back up to the level it started from—at C.

When a wave gets back to the line where it started, it has completed what is known as a *cycle*. If a wave does this twice in a second, we can call it two waves or a wave of two cycles.

That is how all waves are identified; by their number of cycles in a second's time. If we know the number of cycles, this is the same as knowing how often the wave is made. In other words, the number of cycles tells us the *frequency* of the wave.

If the frequency of the wave is not too large, the word *cycle* is very handy to use. But if the frequency is too large, it is not convenient. There is a Greek word that means a thousand; it is *kilo*. So when we want to speak of thousands of cycles we put the two words together to make *kilocycle*.

But often waves are made much faster, and we need still another word. There is a Greek word that means a million; it is *mega*. So when we want to speak of millions of cycles we use *megacycle*.

When we say there are different kinds of waves, we really are saying their frequencies are different.

The frequency of a wave determines what the wave will do and how it can be used. Waves that have a frequency between about 20 cycles and 16,000 cycles are the waves that we hear as sound.

You have heard the sound of thunder. It makes a deep roar. That's because the thunder makes a wave that has a frequency of about 50 cycles a second.

But listen to the cricket behind a barn on a hot summer's night. It makes a little high squeak. That's because the chirp of a cricket makes a wave that has a frequency of 16,000 cycles a second.

A wave of low frequency makes a low sound. A

wave of high frequency makes a high sound. That's why the voice of your father and mother sound different. Your dad's voice has a low frequency; your mother's voice has a high frequency.

When waves have a frequency higher than 16,000 cycles, your ear cannot hear them any more. That is because so many waves are pushing against your eardrum that the drum cannot move back and forth fast enough to keep up with them. The ear just gives up.

But when it comes to making waves, the cricket really is an old slow poke with his chirp. With electricity we can make waves of much higher frequency. In fact, these are the waves we use to send television and radio programs into the air.

Regular radio stations use frequencies between 550,000 and 1,700,000 cycles, or between 550 and 1,700 kilocycles.

Airplanes, ships, and overseas stations use frequencies between 1,700,000 cycles and 30,000,000 cycles, or between 1,700 kilocycles and 30 megacycles.

Television stations use frequencies between 54,000,000 cycles and 216,000,000 cycles, or between 54 and 216 megacycles. These are called *very high frequencies,* or VHF for short.

The newest television stations use frequencies that go up as high as 980,000,000 cycles, or 980 megacycles. These are called *ultra-high frequencies,* or UHF for short.

Perhaps you can guess now how we separate one station from another and always know where to find it.

We give each station its own set of frequencies. You can see how this is done from a chart showing the division of frequencies for television stations operating on Channels 2, 3 and 4.

| Channel Number | Frequency in Megacycles |
|---|---|
| 2 | 54–60 |
| 3 | 60–66 |
| 4 | 66–72 |

Now the job of the station is easy. All it does is make sure that the wave carrying its program to your home is sent out at the right frequency.

Your receiver at home then acts like an electrical post office. It sorts out the waves according to their frequencies and puts each one in its proper box.

When you tune in a station, you open the door to this box and out comes your program. When you want to tune to another station, you close the first box so that the program will not come out any more.

Then you open another box, and out comes your second program.

Just as people's mail comes out of the box when it is opened with the right combination, so the television program can be received only with the right electrical combination. Making the right electrical combination is what you do when you tune your set.

# 8.

# Electronic Merry-Go-Round

It is not hard to make waves of any frequency. All we must do is go back to our old friend—the coil of wire.

You will remember that every time we sent electricity through the coil, the electricity made a wave. If we sent the electricity back and forth many times, we made many waves.

To control the number of waves, or their frequency, all we do is control the number of times that we send the electricity back and forth through the coil.

Let's show the coil and use a wire to connect its two ends as in the picture on the next page.

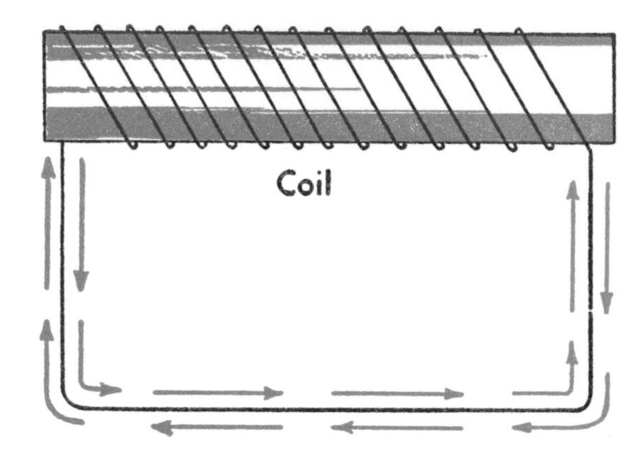


When the electricity goes around the wire and comes to the coil, it finds that it has a long trip ahead. It takes time for the electricity to go around and around the coil until it finally gets through to the other end. Because the electricity goes back and forth slowly, it cannot make very many waves. It wastes too much time getting through the coil.

Now connect a small coil to the wire:

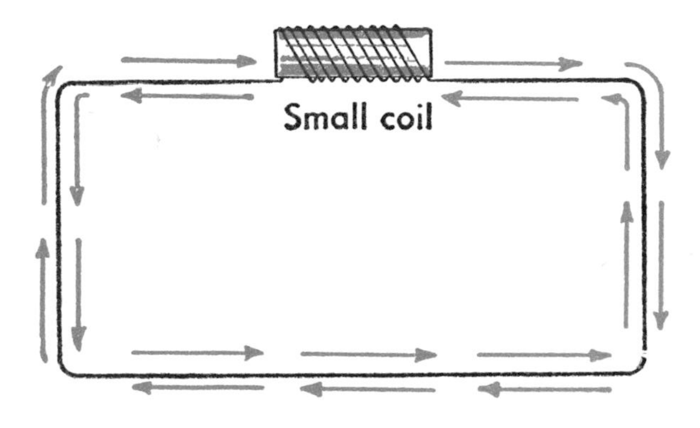

The electricity can get through this coil much more easily. Since it does not have so far to travel, it can go back and forth much more quickly. This means that with the little coil the electricity can make more waves.

If we want to send out a wave of low frequency, we use a big coil. And if we want to send out a wave of high frequency, we use a small coil.

But there is one trouble in using a coil. Often the coil is careless and sloppy and will let more than one wave through. Sometimes in a receiver, a coil will let two waves go through at the same time. Then you hear two programs at once.

We need to help the coil do a better job of controlling the electricity that goes back and forth. To do this we use another device called a *condenser*.

A condenser is made of two metal plates that face each other and are separated by air, like this:

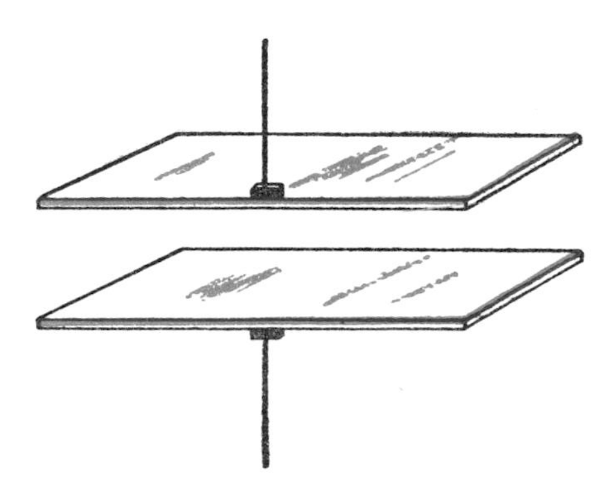

Suppose we connect two plates with a piece of wire so that the condenser looks like this:

When the plates are connected in this way the condenser acts much the same as an egg timer in the shape of an old-fashioned hourglass.

In the hourglass two bowls are connected so that sand can run from one to another. We can call one bowl A and the other B. If the sand is in Bowl A, it starts to run through to Bowl B like this:

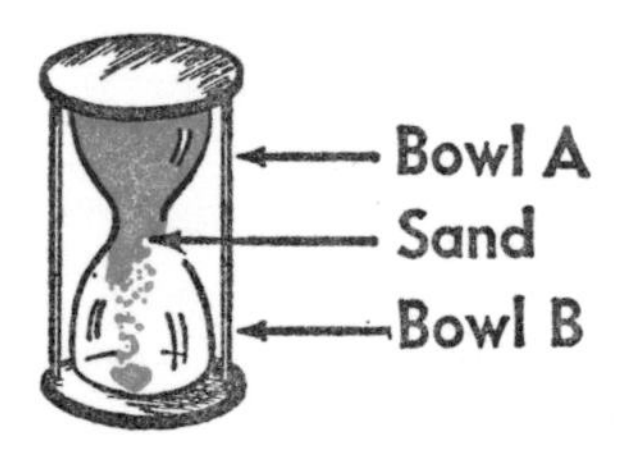


In a couple of minutes the bottom is filled with sand. If we want to keep the sand moving, we must turn the egg timer upside down. Then Bowl B is on top, and the sand starts to run back to Bowl A. Soon all the sand is in Bowl A again.

To keep the sand going back and forth, we must keep turning the egg timer over.

The condenser does to electricity what the egg timer does to the sand. We can label one plate of the condenser A and the other B. Imagine we start with all the electricity on Plate A like this:

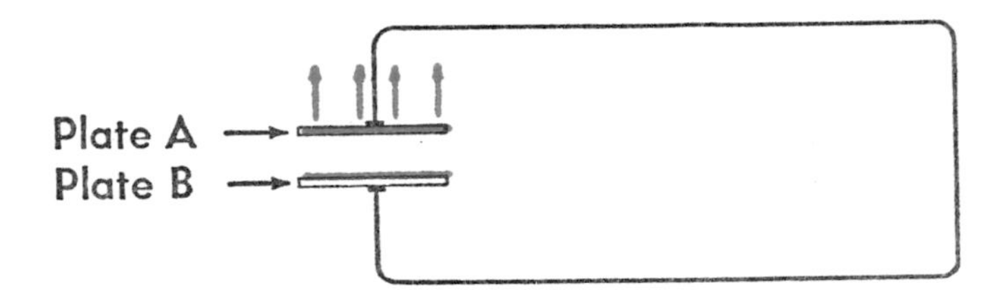


The condenser first lets the electricity leave Plate A and go around the wire toward Plate B like this:

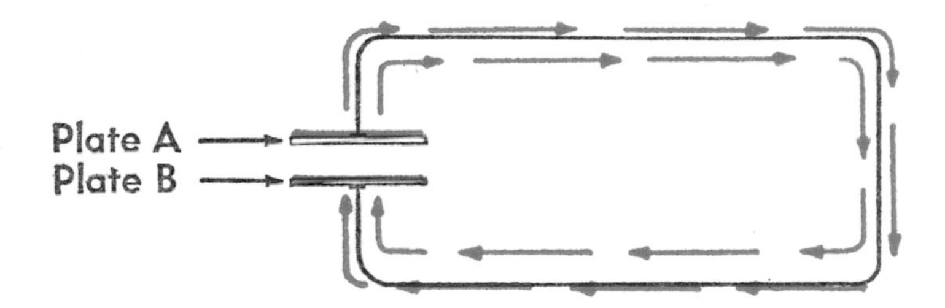


In a fraction of a second all the electricity has left Plate A and is now stored up on Plate B like this:

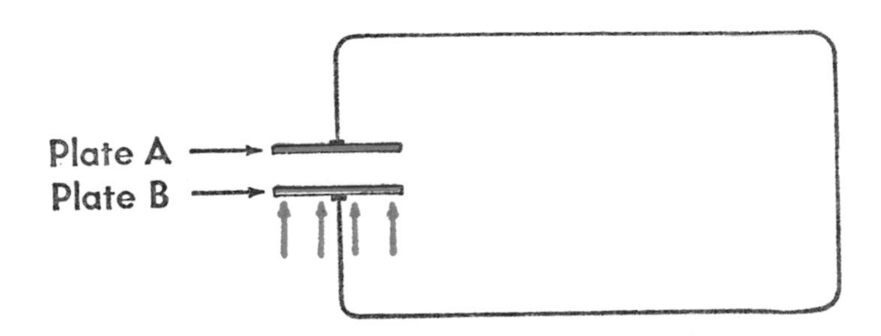

Just as we turned the egg timer over to keep the sand running, the condenser turns the electricity around and it leaves Plate B and starts around back to Plate A like this:

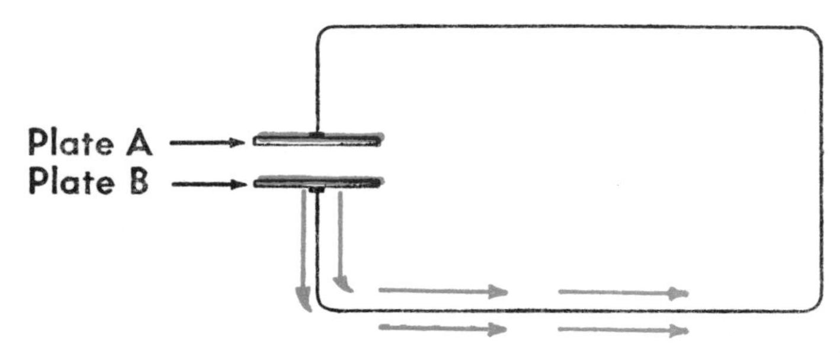


In another second all the electricity is back again on Plate A like this:

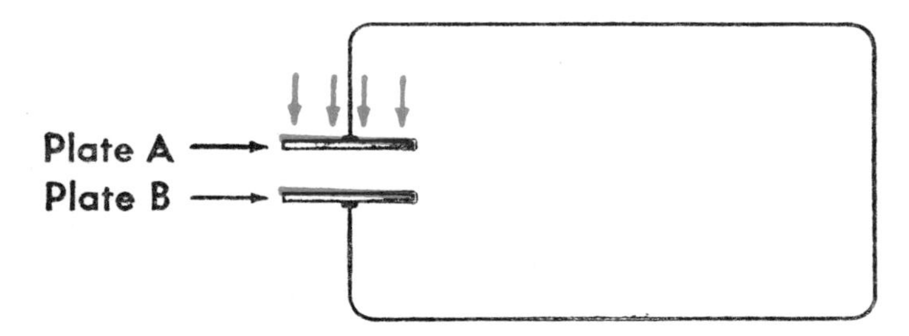


Over and over again the condenser keeps the electricity moving back and forth between Plate A and Plate B.

With the egg timer, it was the size of the bowls, as well as the size of the opening between the bowls, which helped determine how long it took the sand to go from one bowl to another. If the bowls are big, it takes longer to fill them up and empty them. If small, it doesn't take so long. In other words, the size of the bowls helps decide how often we can send the sand back and forth.

In the condenser the plates act the same way. If they are big, the electricity cannot make so many trips back and forth. If small, the electricity can make more round trips.

The size of the coil determined how often electricity would go back and forth. In the same way the size of the condenser does the same thing. Now we have two ways to control the electricity, and this means we have two ways to control the number or frequency of waves.

We connect the coil and the condenser like this:

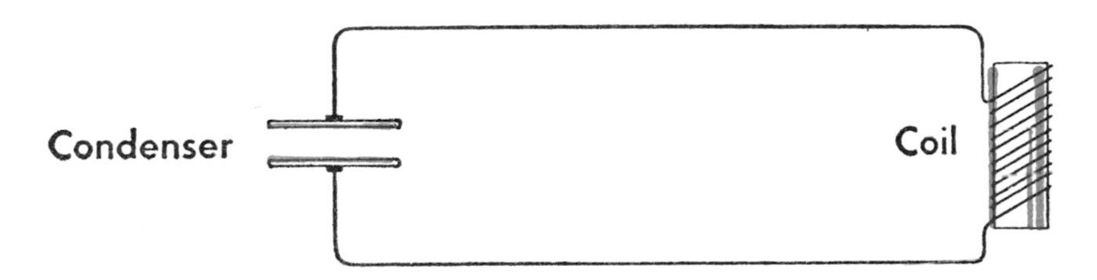


The coil and the condenser give us the electrical combination that we need to pick the right frequency. If the coil slows up the electricity, the condenser keeps it moving. If the condenser slows up the electricity, then the coil keeps it moving. This means that there is always a way to "step on the gas" or "step on the brake." Just as this enables the driver of a car to decide how many times he wants to drive around a block, so it enables us to fix the frequency of a wave.

The electrical combination of a coil and a condenser is used both in the transmitter at the broadcasting station and in the receiver in your home.

At the broadcasting station the combination must be adjusted for only one set of frequencies—the frequencies of the carrier waves that take the station's programs out into the air. Once the adjustment is fixed, we just connect the coil and the condenser to the wire leading up to the transmitter tower.

At the receiver the combination must be adjusted to receive many different frequencies—one group for each station. One way to adjust the combination is to use several coils of different sizes and also a condenser whose size can be changed.

A condenser whose size can be changed is called a *variable condenser*. A variable condenser is made by using two sets of small plates. The plates in each set are hooked together so that the effect is the same as having two big plates.

One set of plates is fastened to a rod—like a small axle—which can be turned. By turning the rod, we vary the position of the plates and make either a big or small reservoir in which to store electricity. This gives us a way to regulate the electricity flowing back and forth between the plates.

Look in back of a radio set while you turn the tuning dial. You can see the plates move in and out like this:

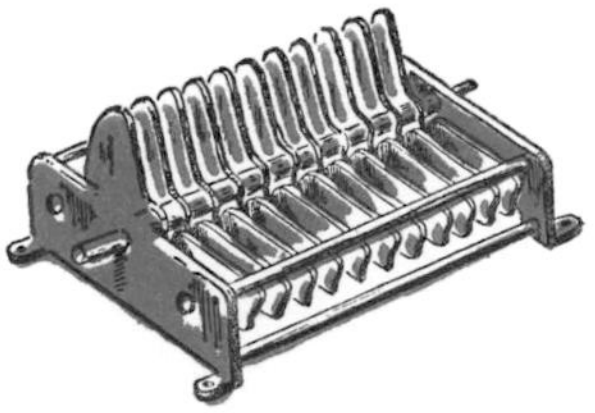

At the receiver we adjust the combination of the coil and the condenser to the frequency of the station we want to receive. When we pick the right frequency, it is like opening a gate for the electricity which is made in the aerial by the carrier waves. The electricity comes down to the coil and the condenser and finds everything ready. It goes right in.

All the other stations with different frequencies find that they are out of step. The electricity made by their waves moves back and forth too often or not often enough. They cannot get in.

# 9.

# How to Build a "Foxhole Radio"

One of the things that makes television and radio interesting is that you can use right away the information you have learned.

We are going to build a radio that is different from any you have seen. In the radio will be these things:

An old safety razor blade
A safety pin
A broken point from a lead pencil

Radios of this kind were actually used during World War II. American G.I.'s in Italy put several of them together. At night when they sat near the front lines, they listened to phonograph records played on a radio station in Rome. That is why the set you are going to make is called "The Foxhole Radio." If you live within twenty-five or thirty miles of a station, you can hear a program on your foxhole radio, too.

These are the only tools you need to build the foxhole radio:

A hammer
A pair of pliers
A pocket knife

These are the parts that you will need:

A board. Any piece of wood will do. Just make sure it is at least eight inches long and six inches wide. It can be bigger if you like.

A piece of cardboard tubing. This should be two inches in diameter, like the tubes on which ribbon is wrapped in five-and-ten-cent stores. The tube should be six inches long.

A spool of insulated copper wire. You may have to buy this at a radio store. Ask for No. 28 gauge; this is just the right size. The wire will cost about 75 cents.

A pair of earphones which you can put over your head like the pilot of a jet airplane. The phones can be bought at a radio store for two or three dollars.

Three new nails. The nails can be either an inch or two inches long. Anything you have will do.

Four metal thumbtacks, not plastic tacks

A used blade that fits a safety razor. A plain white-looking blade often works better than "blue" blades.

A big safety pin

A pencil with a fat lead

Let's put all the tools and parts on a table like this and see if we have everything before we begin:

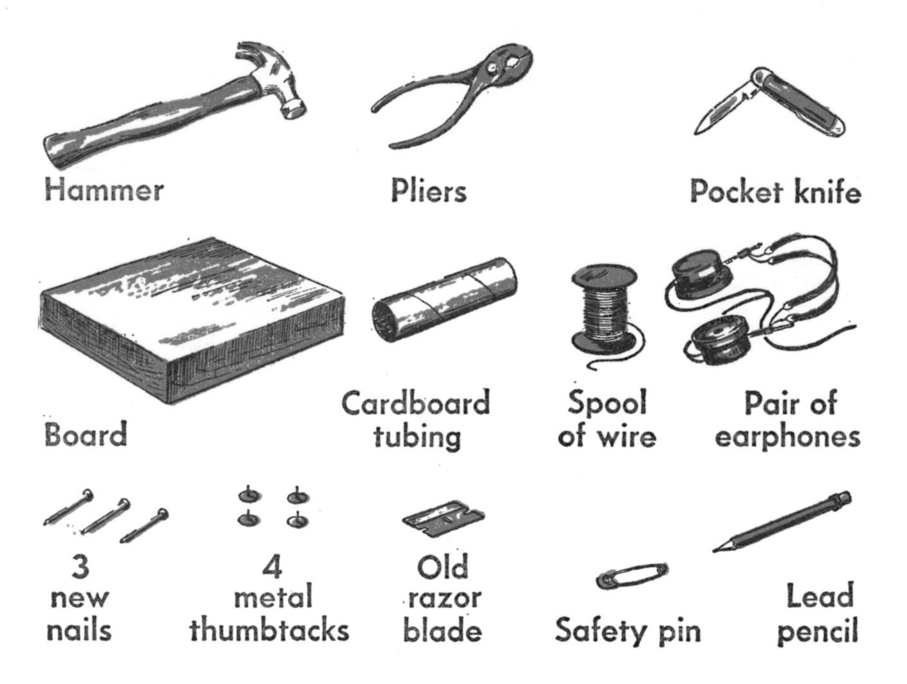


You will need to know how the parts are used and what you must do to make the foxhole radio. This is the way the set looks when it is all finished.

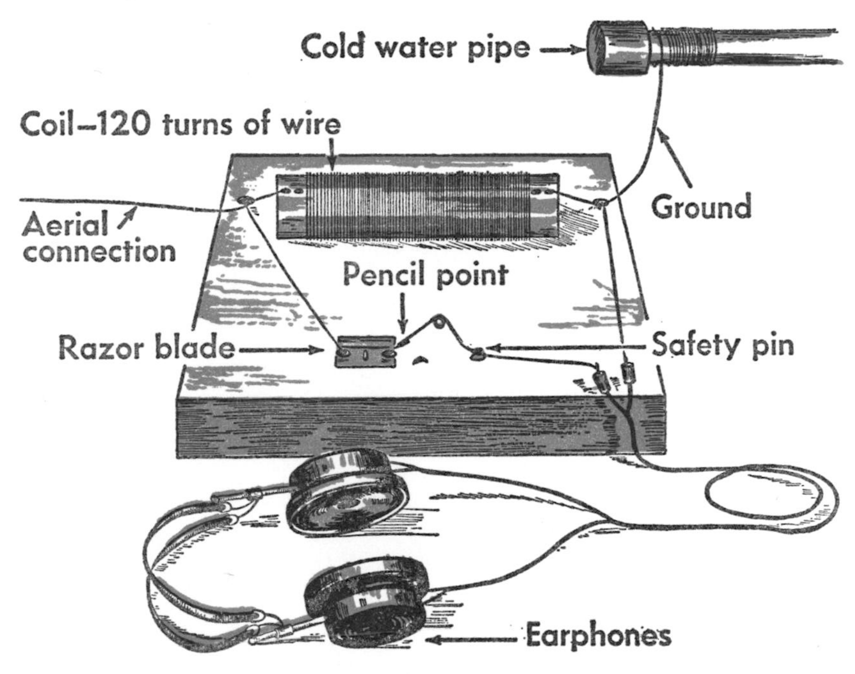


First, we start with the coil.

Unwind a long piece of wire from the spool and stretch it out straight across the floor.

Pick up the piece of cardboard tubing, and with one of the nails make two little holes at one end of the tube and two little holes at the other end. We'll number the holes 1, 2, 3 and 4. Now the tubing looks like this:

Push about six inches of the wire through Hole No. 2. Now pull the wire up through Hole No. 1. You can see that the two holes give us a way to hold the wire in place at one end of the tubing.

Hold the tubing in your left hand. With your right pick up the wire and carefully wind it around and around the tube. Do this until you have a total of 120 turns of wire around the tubing. Make sure the turns lie side by side on the tubing, not one on top of the other.

After you have put 120 turns of wire around the tubing, measure off six inches of wire. Then cut the wire with your pliers. Push the end of the wire down through Hole No. 3 and then pull it up through Hole No. 4. Now you have made a nice sturdy coil that will stay in place.

Put the board in front of you on a table, and lay the coil on its side on the back of the board. Take two of the thumbtacks, and fasten the coil to the board. Make sure the thumbtacks do not touch any part of the wire.

Next put the razor blade in place in front of the coil. Be very careful when you handle the blade; it is sharp. Lay the blade flat on the board, and gently fix it in place with two metal thumbtacks. Do not push the tacks all the way into the board; just start them like this:

Next is the safety pin. First, sharpen the pencil so that you have a long piece of lead showing. Break off the lead, and put it next to the point of the safety pin. Cut a piece of wire off the spool and pull off the cotton covering so that the wire is bare. Now wire the piece of lead to the point of the pin.

With your pliers bend the head of the pin back so that it will lie flat on the board.

Now the safety pin looks like this:

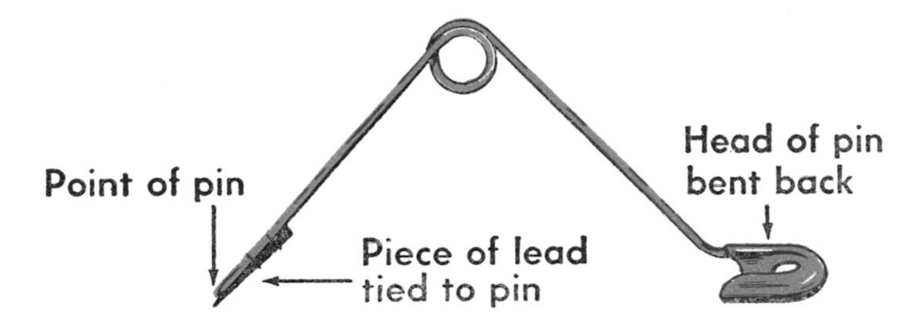


Place the pin to the right of the razor blade. Put one of the nails through the head of the pin, and with the hammer drive the nail into the board until it almost touches the pin.

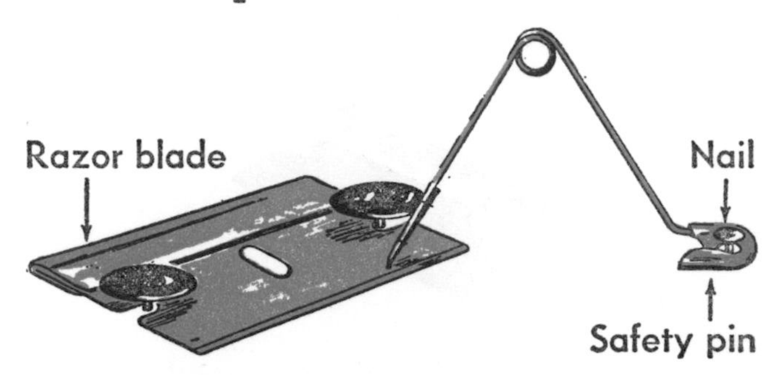


All the parts are in place. Now we hook them together with wires. We do this by using the pocket knife to remove the cotton covering from the ends of the wire so that they are clean and the copper of the wire shines brightly. This is most important because the set will not work without clean, tight connections.

Let's take the left half of the set first:

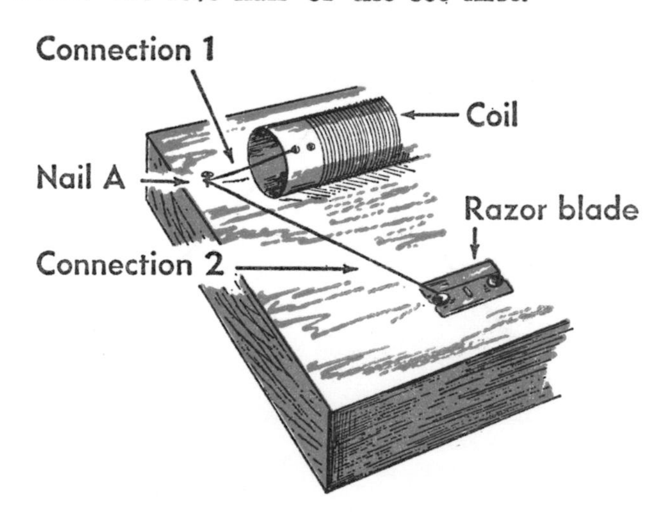

Take the wire from the coil and wrap the bare end around Nail A in the corner. This is Connection No. 1.

Take another wire and put a bare end underneath the thumbtack that holds the razor blade. Push the tack down as hard as you can so that the bare wire is against the blade. Then take the other end of this wire and wrap it around Nail A. This is Connection No. 2.

Now the right half of the set. It looks like this:

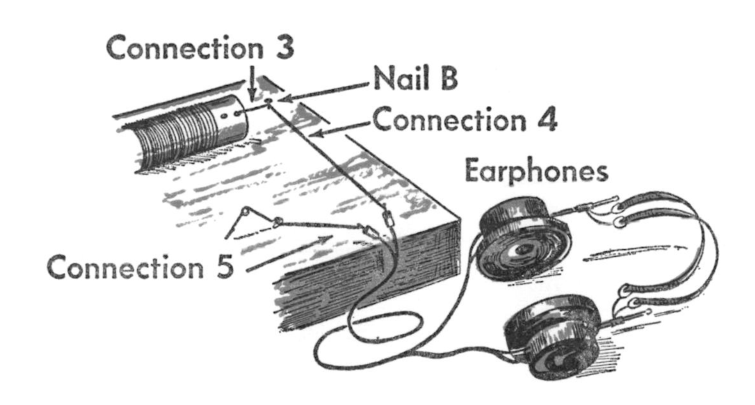


Take the wire from the right end of the coil and wrap it around Nail B in the corner. That is Connection No. 3.

Wrap another wire around the Nail B. Take the other end of this wire and wrap it around one of the metal tips on the cord of the earphones. This is Connection No. 4.

Take another wire and wrap it around the other metal tip of the earphone cord. Now take the other end of this wire and put it under the head of the nail that holds the safety pin. With your hammer then pound this nail in so that the pin will stand up. Don't nail it so tightly that the pin cannot move a little. This is Connection No. 5.

Our set is finished! But to make it work there are still two more things we must do.

First, we must have an aerial wire which the waves can cross and make electricity go back and forth into our coil. Whatever aerial you use, wrap one end of it around Nail A that connects with the coil and razor blade.

The longer the aerial the better. That will make more electricity move into the coil. You can use the wire that still is left on the spool and let it dangle out of a window. Or, better yet, perhaps you can get fifty or a hundred feet of any kind of wire and string it from a window to a tree out in the yard.

We also must have a connection to something that goes into the ground. The best ground connection is a cold water pipe. Take another piece of wire, scrape off the cotton covering and wind it tightly around a pipe. Take the other end of this wire and wrap it around Nail B.

With the aerial and the ground connected, we are all ready to get a program! Remember, a foxhole radio is different from the average set. So do not expect to hear music and voices booming in right away.

Put on the earphones, and do not make any noise in the room where you have your set. With your finger move the pin very gently so that the little piece of lead goes across the razor blade. Try putting the tip of the lead where the manufacturer of the blade has put his name.

Suddenly you will hear very faint little crackly noises in your earphones. Be careful. A station may come in at any moment. Move the pin just a shade more. Listen! There is somebody talking. Don't move the pin. If you do, you may lose the station. Listen again. Do you hear two voices? You should not be surprised. Remember, we learned that a coil all by itself sometimes will let two programs come in.

A foxhole radio is a lot of fun. But why does it work?

Well, we know the incoming waves send electricity back and forth in the coil. But we know we must fix this electricity so that its changes will go in only one direction into our earphones.

The safety razor blade and the piece of lead act like an electrical gate. The blade is made of steel and the pencil point is made of carbon. When the steel and carbon touch each other, they will let electricity go through in only one direction. Once the electricity gets through the razor blade and the safety pin, it goes into our earphones.

But one of the most interesting things about radio is that if we can do something one way, we often can do it another way.

Let's see if we can improve our foxhole radio. We can very easily. We can change it into a crystal radio set. To do this we must go to a radio store and buy a *crystal detector*. It will cost about $1.00.

There are two main parts to a crystal detector. One part is a piece of crystal. This is a mineral called *galena*. The crystal is placed in a little holder which is hooked up to a post. This post is used to make a connection. The crystal takes the place of the razor blade.

The other part of the crystal detector is called a *cat whisker* and takes the place of the safety pin. The cat whisker is mounted on a little arm that we can move just as we moved the safety pin. The cat whisker is also hooked to a post where we can make a connection.

This is the way the crystal and the cat whisker look:

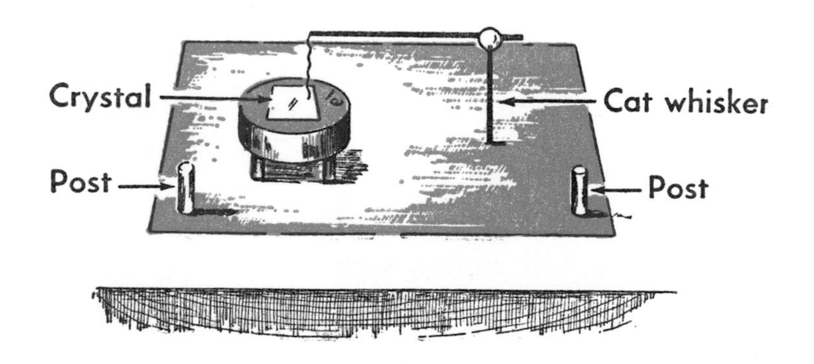

This is how our radio set looks after we have taken out the razor blade and safety pin and put in the crystal:

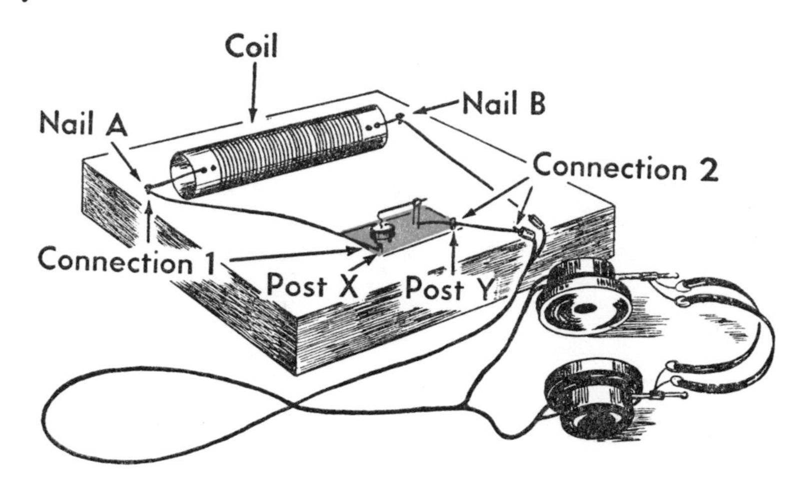


A wire goes from Nail A to Post X on the crystal detector. This is Connection No. 1.

A second wire goes from one of the tips of the earphones to Post Y on the crystal detector. This is Connection No. 2.

To make the crystal work, you must also hook it up to an aerial and a ground connection just as we did with the foxhole radio. Then you grasp the arm of the cat whisker and move it gently so that the end of the fine wire touches the face of the crystal. Listen carefully, and you will find a spot on the crystal which brings in a station best.

It is the crystal which acts like an electrical gate that lets electricity go through in only one direction.

Remember how we said that the combination of a coil and a condenser enabled us to get the station we wanted to hear and keep out those we did not want to hear.

We can add a *variable condenser* to our crystal set, and it will help to separate stations. The condenser also must be bought in a radio store. It costs about $1.50. The size you want has twenty-one plates, some of which turn and some of which are fixed. However, a condenser of either seventeen or nineteen plates will work all right.

This is how the condenser looks when it is put in the set:

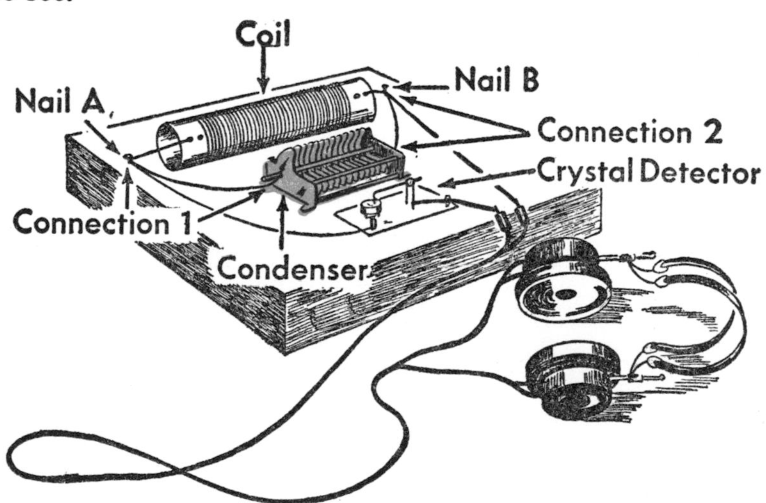

One post on the condenser is connected to the plates that are fixed. From this post a wire is run to Nail A. This is Connection No. 1.

Another post on the condenser is connected to the plates that turn. From this post a wire is run to Nail B. This is Connection No. 2.

With the condenser in the set, we must first move the end of the cat whisker over the top of the crystal until we hear a program. Then we turn the condenser either to the right or left until the sound is heard the loudest.

There is no thrill quite like hearing a program on a set that you have made yourself. But you can see that there are many disadvantages to the foxhole radio and a crystal set. They cannot pick up all the stations you want to hear. They will not work if you are a long distance from a station. And they bring in a station only just loud enough to hear on earphones.

Neither television nor radio as we know them today would be possible if we could not make stations and receivers very powerful. Let's see how we make them powerful.

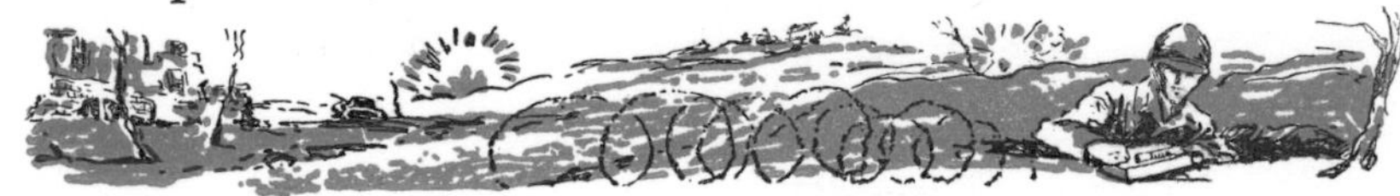

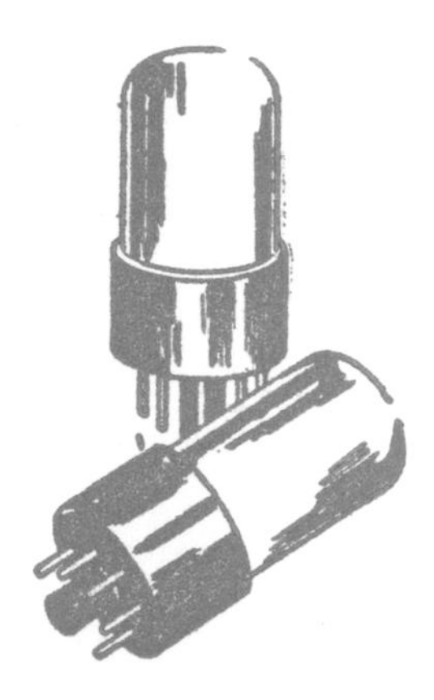

# 10.

# The Vacuum Tube and Transistor

Television and radio sets are made powerful by a wonderful invention. It is the *vacuum tube.*

Tubes are used to do almost everything. They can make a feeble whisper so loud that you can hear it blocks away. They are used to take the place of a crystal. They are used to send waves into the air that may travel hundreds and hundreds of miles.

How a tube works is simple to understand if we know a little more about electricity.

You have seen a current of water run down a river or a brook. A current of electricity acts in very much the same way.

Every current of water actually consists of millions and millions of tiny little drops of water. A current of electricity consists of billions and billions of little tiny particles of electricity. These particles are called *electrons.*

The passage of electrons along a wire makes an electric current. But there is something even more important about an electron. It behaves in a very funny way, and this funny behavior is the secret to the operation of the vacuum tube.

One electron has absolutely no use for another electron. When they come together, they push each other away. The reason for this is that electrons have the same kind of charge of electricity—a negative charge. Charges of electricity which are alike push away from each other.

Also, there is another kind of charge of electricity—a positive charge. A positive charge is called a *proton.* An electron is attracted to a proton. Bring them near each other, and the electron will rush to the proton. The reason for this is that unlike charges of electricity attract each other.

In other words, electrons will move faster if they

can be attracted by positive charges of electricity. And electrons can be slowed down by putting negative charges in their way.

What the vacuum tube does first is make a supply of electrons. Then by controlling the electrons in different ways a tube does different things.

The outside of a tube is either a glass bulb or a metal shell from which all air has been removed. Tubes come in many different sizes. Some are no bigger than your little finger. Others are so big that it is hard for a man to carry one alone.

Inside every tube, whether big or small, are different kinds of wires and pieces of metal. These are connected to pins in the base of the tube. Through these pins we can send electricity into a tube or take it out.

Let's see what happens when we send electricity into a tube.

One of the wires inside the glass bulb starts to warm up. Soon it will be red hot like a wire in an electric toaster. This wire, called a *filament,* is made of metal, and all metals contain electrons. Some metals, such as tungsten, release electrons as they are heated.

In the radio tube, heat causes electrons to shoot off the wire in clouds like this:

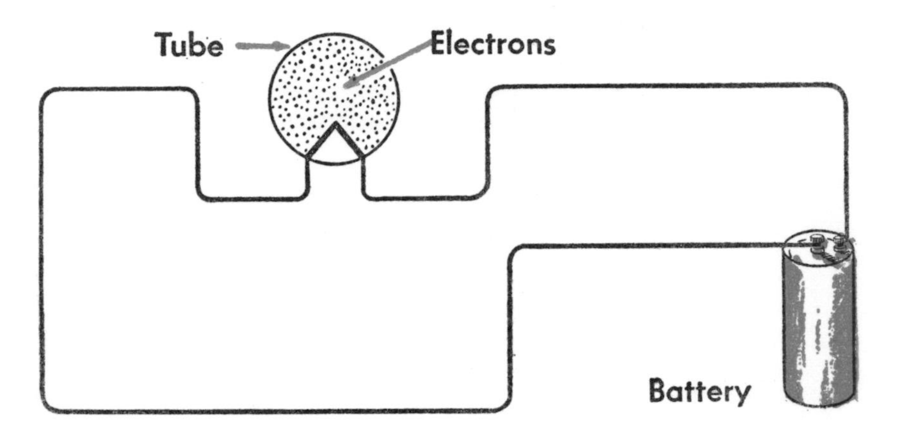


Since the electrons have no place to go inside the tube, they are not of any use. But, if we put a little plate of metal inside the tube, we can make them very useful. Now our tube looks like this:

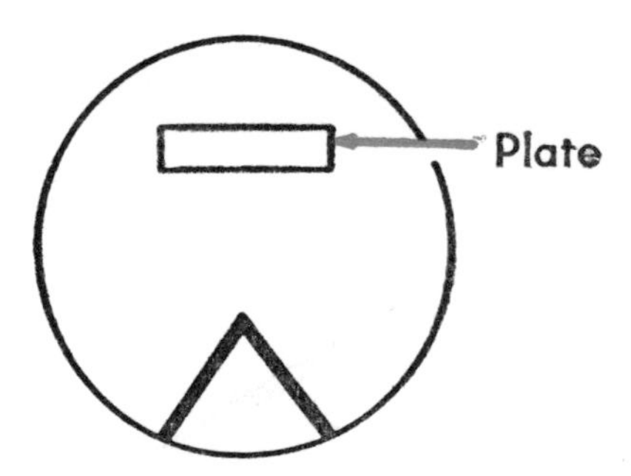


First, suppose we put a positive, or plus, charge of electricity on the plate. That means the plate will attract electrons because electrons are negative charges.

So the electrons rush over to the plate. In other words, there will be a flow of electrons, or a flow of electricity, which looks like this:

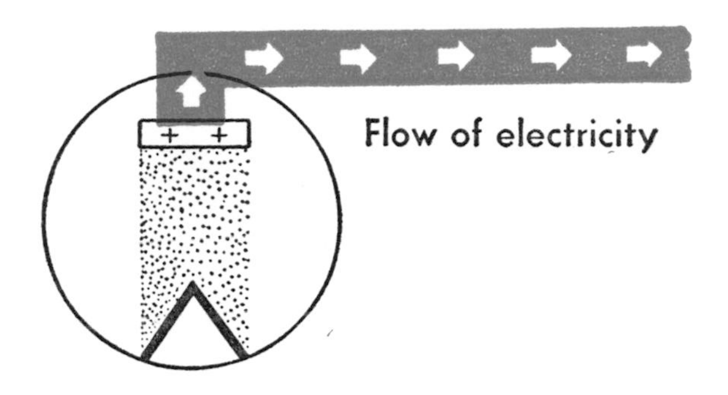


Now suppose we put a negative, or minus, charge on the plate. The electrons will not want to go to the plate. In fact, the plate itself will push away any new electrons. Now there is no flow of electricity as can be seen in this drawing:

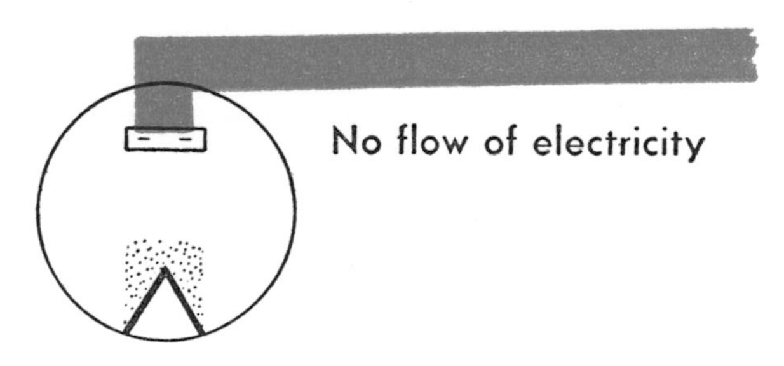


You can see what this kind of tube does. It lets electricity pass in only one direction, just as the razor blade and safety pin or the piece of crystal. All modern television and radio sets use tubes in this way to separate sound and picture signals from carrier waves. These tubes then are known as *detectors*.

Let's see what happens if we put a wire screen—called a *grid*—inside the tube between the source of the electrons and the plate. Our tube looks like this:

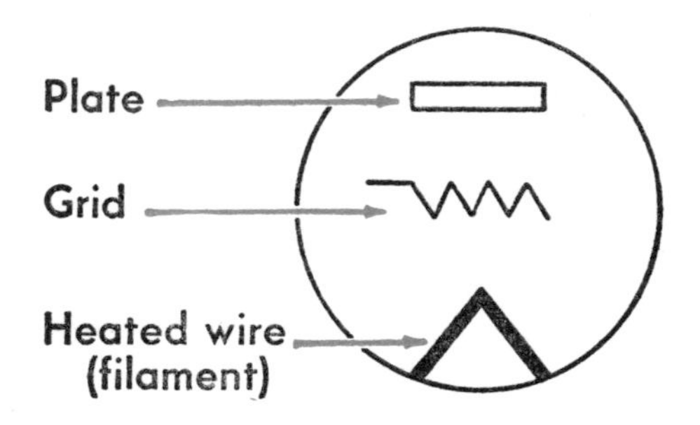


If we put a positive charge of electricity on the grid, it will help attract electrons from the heated wire and speed up the flow to the plate like this:

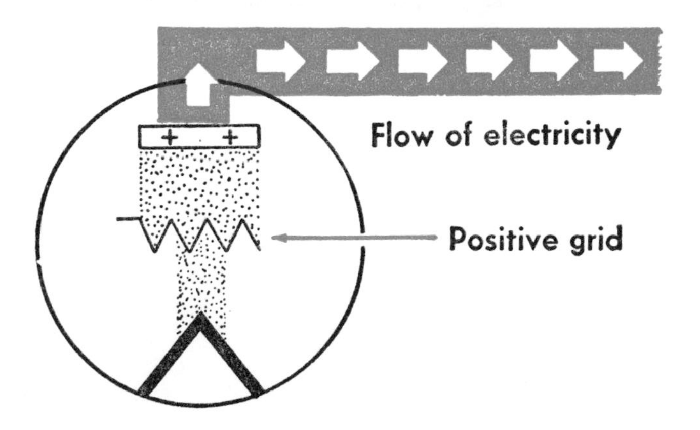

Now suppose we put a negative charge of electricity on the grid. Remember that an electron doesn't like a negative charge. This charge will try to stop the flow from the heated wire. This means less current will flow through the plate like this:

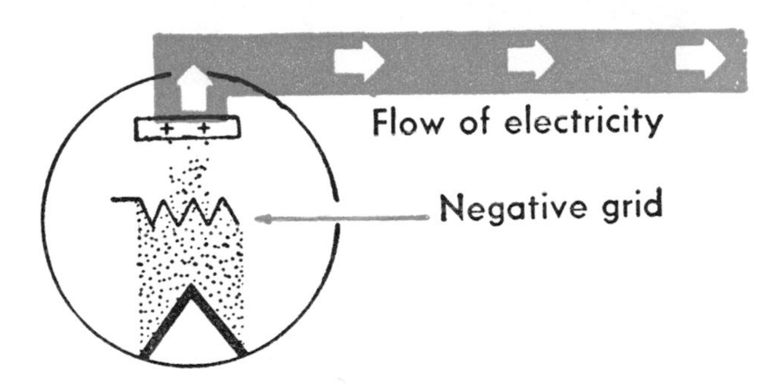


Because the grid can control the flow of electrons through the plate, we can use this tube to increase the strength of a signal. Such a tube is called an *amplifier*. This is how the amplifier works.

Remember when we listened to the foxhole radio how weak the programs sounded? This was because the incoming waves made only very weak electricity in the set.

Let's show this weak electricity with little arrows like this:

But on the plate of our amplifying tube we can use very strong electricity to make the positive charge. We hook up the plate to a source of strong electricity such as we might take from a battery. We can show this electricity with big arrows:

So when we hook up an amplifying tube we really can show it like this:

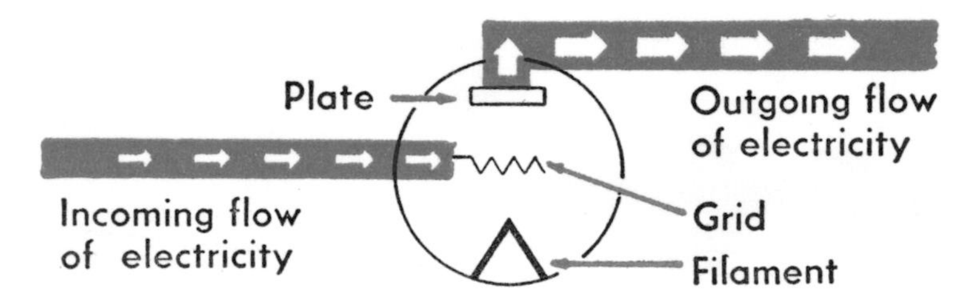


Suppose we want to amplify the loud HI and the soft *ho* that are spoken into a microphone.

This means the weak electricity will show first a big change and then a little change going into the grid like this:

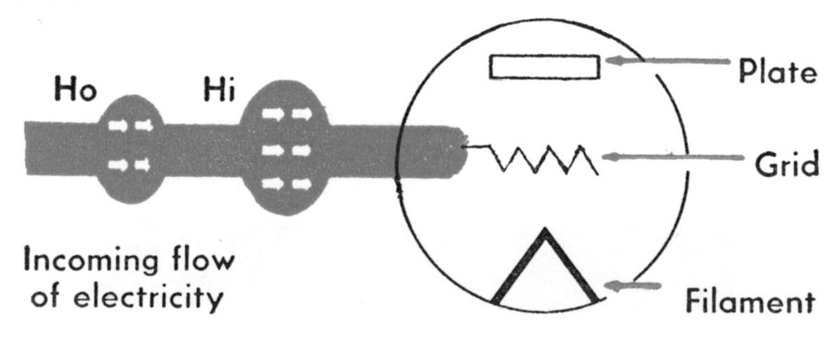

Each change will vary the charge on the grid. First, there will be a big charge, then a little charge.

The big charge will make a big change in the strong plate current and the little charge a little change in the plate current. But since the plate current is so much stronger than the current going into the grid, this is how the HI and the *ho* look when they come out of the tube:

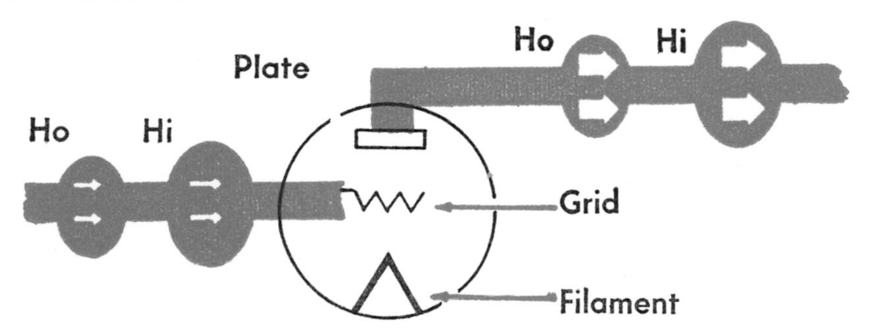


You can see that the amplifying tube really acts like a set of electrical gears. The signal coming into the grid is the little wheel, and the signal going out of the plate is the big wheel.

If we want to make the signal stronger and stronger, all we do is send it step by step through several amplifying tubes. Amplifying tubes are used at broadcasting stations to increase the strength of signals before they are sent out on the air. Then more amplifying tubes are used again to strengthen the weak signals picked up by a receiver.

This is why different kinds of sets have different numbers of tubes. If you just want to listen to radio programs from stations nearby, four or five tubes may be all you need. But if you want to hear very weak signals from stations all over the world, you may need ten or fifteen tubes.

Since television sets must provide both pictures and sound, they use more tubes than radio sets. Some television sets use as many as thirty tubes.

There is another very important use for the amplifying tube. That is to make the carrier waves which take the sound and picture signals through the air.

When we send electricity back and forth through the coil and the condenser, we must have something that will make sure there is always enough electricity. A swing on the playground will stop if someone doesn't keep pushing it. In the same way the electricity will stop if it doesn't receive a push. The amplifying tube gives it the push.

We do this by taking some of the strong electricity from the plate and feeding it back to the coil and the condenser. This makes stronger electricity going into the grid which means still stronger electricity will come out of the plate.

Again and again this is repeated until not only is the electricity kept moving back and forth through the coil and condenser but is made stronger and stronger. After a while, it is powerful enough to make the trip up the wire to the transmitter tower. There it moves back and forth and makes the waves that go out into space.

You can see now why this kind of tube is regarded as one of the greatest achievements of science. It acts like a sort of perpetual motion machine.

But science never stands still; already there is a device which is taking the place of the vacuum tube. It is called the *transistor.*

A transistor can amplify and oscillate just like a tube and do it more easily and in much less space. In a tube electrons move through a vacuum; in a transistor electrons move through solid materials, such as germanium or silicon.

Sometimes a transistor material will have extra electrons. With a nudge these electrons can be made to move from one place to another. Another transistor material may have a shortage of electrons; these are called "holes." By applying a small voltage to the transistor, one electron can be set loose and it will jump into the nearest "hole." Another electron will take its place. Soon we have a procession of electrons—a flow, in other words—moving from hole to hole.

The advantage of the transistor is that it has no filament to burn out. Instead of a filament there is a connection called the *emitter*. Taking the place of the grid in the tube is the *base*. Instead of a plate there is a *collector*. A transistor looks like this:

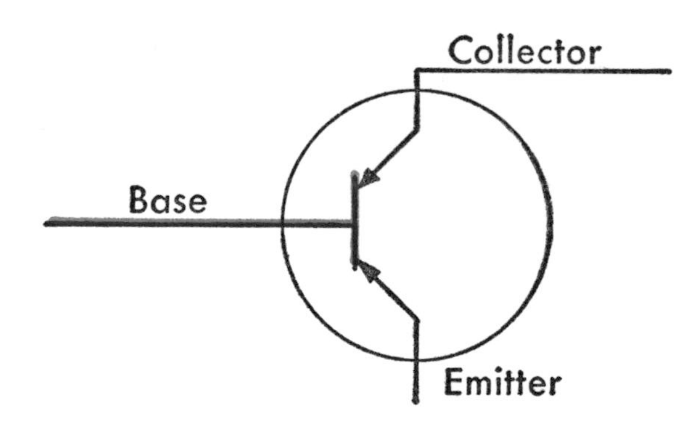


A transistor requires little power to work a long time. A regular tube radio usually needs at least 90 volts to fill a room with music; a transistor radio needs nine volts. Because a transistor is so small—smaller than the nail on your thumb—it is possible to build miniature receivers and transmitters. Transistor radios, powered by energy from the sun, will be put inside earth satellites. The transistor has made the "Dick Tracy" radio a reality; today a small receiver can be strapped around your wrist.

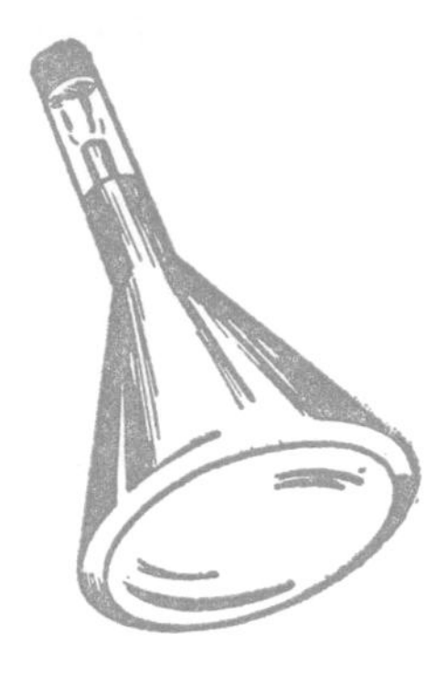

# 11.

# Television Tubes

For television we must use great big vacuum tubes. You yourself know how big some of them are by looking at the size of the screen on your set. The first television sets had tubes that were only seven inches across the face. Now some tubes are thirty-two inches—almost a full yard—from one side to another.

To send and receive television programs we use two kinds of tubes. One is the camera tube and the other is called simply the picture tube—the tube that you watch when you look at your set.

Let's start with the tube in the camera. You recall that we said we change all the black and white dots in a picture into big and little changes of electricity. Now that we know something about electrons we can understand how the tube performs this miracle.

In the face of the camera tube there is a plate. On the plate are hundreds and hundreds of little dots of silver. Over the silver dots is put a metallic compound called *caesium oxide.*

The caesium is what makes the camera tube start to work. When light hits caesium, the caesium sends out a burst of electrons. As the light in the television hits the hundreds and hundreds of small dots of caesium, we have hundreds and hundreds of bursts of electrons. Where the light is bright, the caesium sends out a lot of electrons; where the light is dark, the caesium sends out few electrons.

What we must do now is collect all these little bursts of electrons—one by one—so that we can use them to control the carrier waves that are sent out from the transmitting tower.

To do this an "electronic gun" is put inside the tube. The easiest way to understand how the "gun" works is to think of it as a long spyglass.

The spyglass starts in the upper left-hand corner of the picture and sweeps straight across to the upper right-hand corner. Then the spyglass is brought a little lower, and again it sweeps from left to right. Again and again, it sweeps from left to right until it has gone down the picture line by line, just as you have read this page line by line.

What we've really done is to cut the picture into thin strips so that they look like this:

But the television camera does not divide the picture into just a few strips. It divides the picture into 525 lines and goes over each line thirty times in a second.

As the spyglass goes over the lines, it collects the big and little bursts of electrons and sends them on a wire in one continuous ribbon.

Imagine, for example, if the following sports bulletin were painted on a card and held up in front of a camera like this:

JOHNNY JONES
HIT A HOME
RUN WITH THREE
MEN ON BASE.

The "gun," in effect, does not pick up all four lines at once as your eye does. Instead it picks them up as one long line like this:

JOHNNY JONES HIT A HOME RUN WITH THREE MEN ON BASE.

Now we have a current of electricity that has big and little changes for the black and white dots in the picture. But where the caesium sent out a big burst of electrons for a bright dot and a small burst for a black dot, the "gun" sends its changes the other way around—a big change for a black dot and a small change for a white dot.

These changes are used to modulate or shape the

waves sent out by the station. Then the waves make the same kind of changes that show up in the receiver. Since we are dealing with electricity, these changes can be sent through little tubes to be detected or amplified just as changes made by a microphone.

When the changes reach the picture tube of your receiver, they come to another "electronic gun." But instead of collecting electrons, this "gun" shoots out bursts of electrons. And on the face of the tube in the receiver are hundreds and hundreds of little bits of a material called *phosphor*. When a bit of phosphor is hit by a burst of electrons, it gives off light—a dark or bright light depending on whether it is hit by a big or little burst.

The "gun" of the picture tube takes the incoming ribbon of changes in electricity and shoots it across the bits of phosphor. As the "gun" goes over the face of the tube, line by line, one phosphor after another lights up. This puts into the picture all the black and white dots.

Since the "gun" in the picture tube is moving in step with the "gun" in the camera tube, the sports bulletin is reproduced on your screen at home just as it was seen in the studio:

JOHNNY JONES
HITS A HOME
RUN WITH THREE
MEN ON BASE.

The two "guns"—one in the camera tube and one in the picture tube—really work like two windshield wipers that go back and forth together on the front window of a car. The only difference is that in television they move so fast you do not even know they are working. Whatever the camera sees in the studio, you see at home.

# 12.

# Color Television

If sending black-and-white pictures through the air seems wonderful, hold your breath! There is an even greater wonder—television in full color.

Color television gives your eye much more information than television in black and white. Imagine a forward pass in a football game. Suppose two or three players are in the same spot and one jumps up and grabs the ball.

With black-and-white television your eye cannot always tell whether it was a completed pass or whether the pass was intercepted by a member of the other team. But in color television, if one player's uniform is red and the other's green, there is no uncertainty.

Or take baseball. You must stop to realize how much you miss when you see a game only in black and white. You miss the green grass, the white baseball, the light brown bat, the dark brown dirt, the light blue sky and the dark blue uniform of the umpire. We are so accustomed to color that we take it for granted.

There are three main colors in color television—red, blue and green. These are the primary colors which are used to make all the other colors. Television's primary colors are different from those used in mixing paints, which are red, blue and yellow.

With paints you mix blue and yellow to make green. But with television you use red and green to make yellow. If you mix red, blue and green in equal parts, you get white in color television.

The colors themselves are not sent through the air. Instead, at the color television station, we change the color picture into three different currents of electricity—one for each color. These currents, each with its own changes of electricity for bright and dark parts of the picture, are then used to shape the waves that go out into space, just as in black-and-white television.

At the color broadcasting station, one color is

separated from another color by filters which are like little windowpanes. There are three windows—one for each color. Only red colors can go through the red window; only blue through the blue window and only green through the green window.

Back of the three windowpanes there are three camera tubes. As the red color comes through the red window, it goes to its own tube, where it makes its own big and little changes in electricity. The green color does the same to the second tube, and the blue to the third tube.

Once we have the three sets of changes, we use them one after the other to shape the carrier wave. This means that the picture is still sliced up into strips, as in black and white television, but each strip contains red, blue and green colors.

At the receiver, the changes of electricity for each strip are fed into the "gun" of the receiving tube. Built into the face of the tube are color phosphors. These give off red, blue or green colors when hit by the bursts of electrons. As in black-and-white television, the "gun" goes over the picture line by line. Finally, all the colors are put together just as they were seen at the studio.

## Color Television

Color television is more complicated than black-and-white television because there must be separate signals for each of the three colors. That is why black-and-white television came first.

With the newest system of color television the same picture is really sent out in two ways—in black-and-white and in color. The color carrier wave, it could be said, is hooked on to the black-and-white carrier wave, much as a bomb is hooked underneath an airplane.

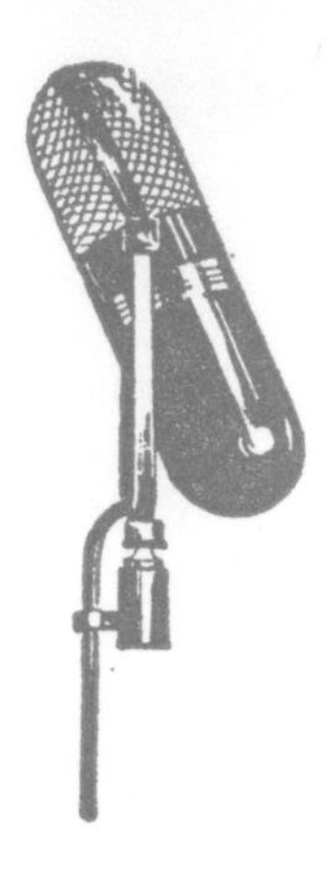

# 13.

# Why We Have Television Networks

Television would not be much fun to watch if there were no way to send programs over long distances.

When the New York Yankees go on the diamond to play in a World Series, baseball fans all over the country want to see the game at the same time. If two funny clowns in Hollywood make people laugh, boys and girls in Florida and Texas want to see them just as do boys and girls in New England and Oregon.

It would be wonderful if we could put up just one great big television station in the middle of the United States and then send out big circles of waves all over the country. But we cannot do that. Television waves do not travel very far before they die out.

To understand how far a television wave can travel, we must learn something new about waves—the length of waves. We can easily tell about the length of waves by going back to the rope tied to the doorknob.

Give the rope a shake like this:

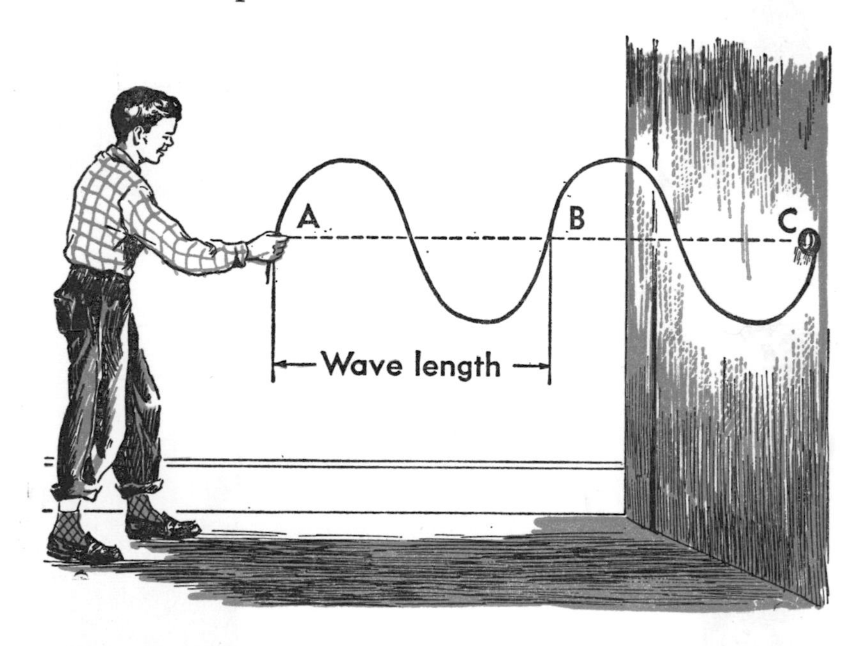


You can see that the length of the wave is the distance from A to B, or from B to C.

Whether the length of a wave is long or short depends on how often we send out the waves. Imagine that first we make two waves with the rope like this:

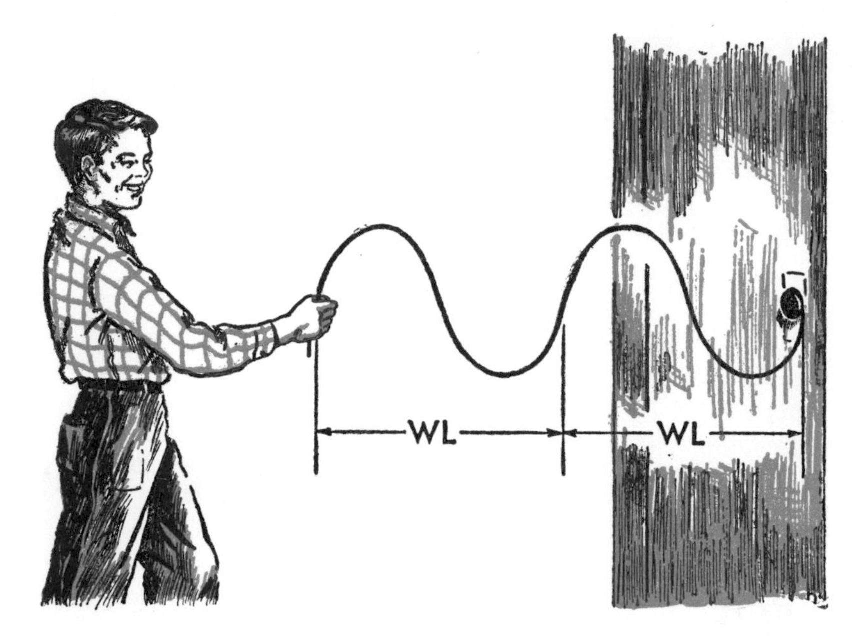


And then we make four waves, like this:

With only two waves the wave length is twice as great as with four waves.

In other words, it is the frequency of the waves which determines their length. If the waves have a high frequency, then their length is short. If they have a low frequency, then their length is long.

So when we talk about the length of a wave and the frequency of a wave, we are talking about almost the same thing. It is just another way of telling one wave from another.

It is the length of a wave which decides how far it will go. Waves of different lengths will travel different distances. Some will go very far out into space; others will go only a short distance.

Television waves are very short because their frequencies are so high. When millions and millions of waves are sent out every second, their length can be measured in feet or inches.

When the length of the waves is so short, they travel only about as far as you can see.

You know that if you climb to the top of a mountain you can see much farther than when you are standing on the ground. It is for the same reason that the transmitting towers of television stations are put on the top of a mountain or on the top of tall buildings, like the Empire State Building in New York.

The higher the tower is, the farther the waves can go out and carry programs to people living over a wider area like this:

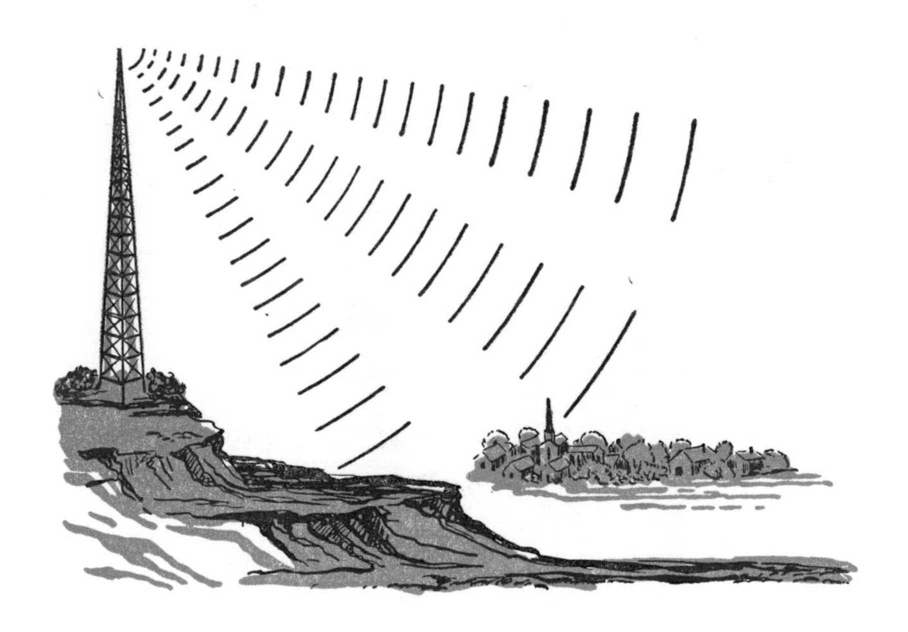

But even if you are on top of a high building, there is a limit to how far you can see. Sooner or later your eyes see only the horizon.

Most TV waves have the same limitation as your

eyes. They cannot go beyond the horizon. This means that, depending on the height of the transmitting tower, they cannot travel beyond fifty to a hundred miles. After that they just die out like the waves we made by dropping a rock into a pond.

People try to put their aerials up as high as they can so they can pick up strong signals. But if you live near a television station, the waves may be so strong that you only need an indoor aerial.

Sometimes you may look at a television set and see everything twice like this:

It looks as if you were not only seeing the man's face but his ghost.

"Ghosts" are made in a television set when the waves

travel to the set from two different directions like this:

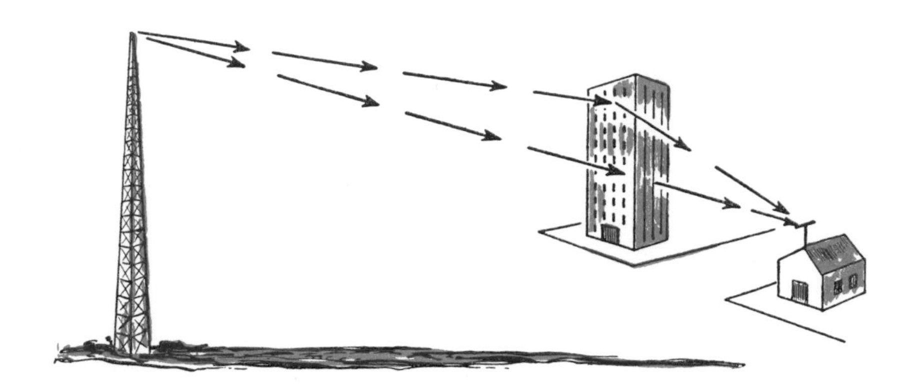

One wave has gone directly to the set. That wave carries the strong picture you see.

The other wave hits the office building and then bounces over to the set. That's the "ghost."

The reason you see two pictures is because the waves do not arrive at the set at the same moment. The wave carrying the strong picture gets to the set first because it takes a direct route. But the other wave must make a longer trip so it arrives a fraction of a second later. That's why you see first one picture of the man and then the other.

Because each television station can send its own waves only about fifty to a hundred miles, we must find another way to carry programs over greater distances.

We do this very simply—we connect one station to another. Then both stations can carry the same program at the same time. We can keep adding more and more stations until we have a big network of stations that stretches from New York to California. Each station is a link in the chain.

A network is not put together the way you may think: one station broadcasting a program to a second station, and a second to a third. The reason is that many of the broadcasting stations are much too far apart.

There are two ways to connect television stations. One way is by means of a cable, called a *coaxial cable.* This is just a wire inside tubing that looks like a fire hose. This cable is laid under the ground and runs from one city to another. When not used for television, the same cable can carry hundreds of long-distance telephone calls all at the same time.

The newer way to connect stations is called a *radio relay*. A radio relay actually is a long line of baby receivers and baby transmitters.

The first link in a relay sends out the program just like a television station. Thirty miles away there is another link. This receives the program, sends it through amplifying tubes to boost its strength, and then sends it on its way to the next link. Again and again this is done every thirty miles until the program gets to its destination.

Across the United States there are over a hundred of these relays spread out like this:

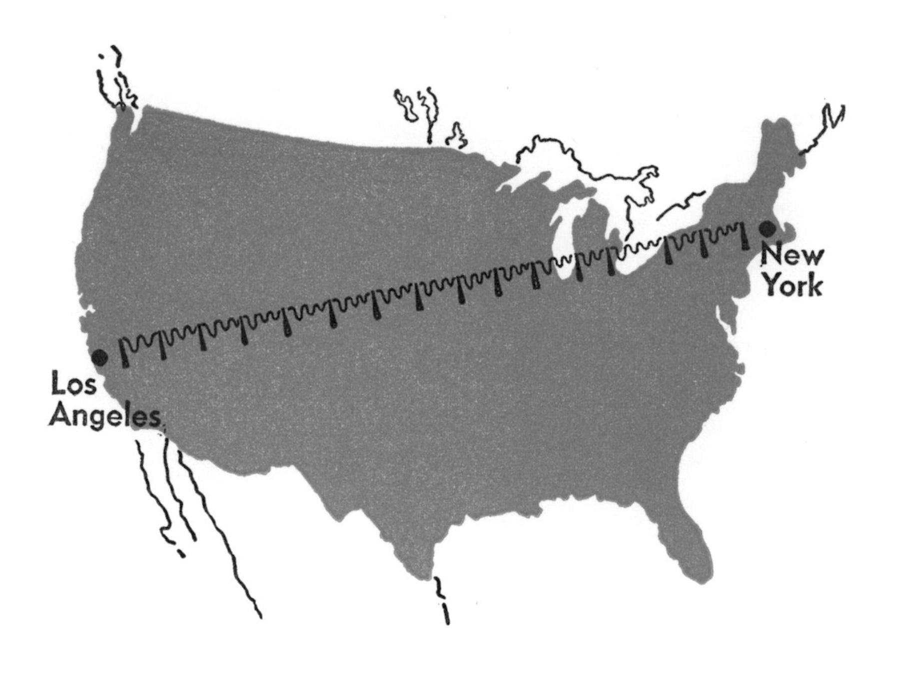


To make sure that strong signals are sent along the whole route engineers had to put some of the relay links on top of tall office buildings in big cities, others on the lonely and empty desert of the West, and others over the Rocky Mountains.

At any point along the coaxial cable or the relay, an individual station can be hooked into the network. Actually, there are several networks all running at the same time so that people in many different cities can have a choice of more than one program.

Television networks at first were constructed over large areas of land; in Europe a network connects Denmark and Sicily and England and Czechoslovakia. It is known as "Eurovision." But engineers are beginning to span long distances over water; Cuba now can send programs to the United States.

Scientists have found that by sending extremely powerful television signals up to the sky some of these signals will come back to the earth three hundred miles away. This scattering of signals then can be picked up on very sensitive receivers. These receivers are much more complicated than you would need in your home.

This system of transmission is known as "scatter propagation." It makes possible the sending of pictures "over the horizon." If there were relay stations in Maine, Newfoundland, Labrador, Greenland,

Iceland, Ireland and Scotland, a United States television network could be connected to Eurovision.

# 14.

# Why Radio Can Go Around the World

When it comes to sending a radio program out into the air, we are lucky. We have a choice of many different waves—some long, some short, and some very short, like television waves.

With their many different lengths, radio waves will travel many distances. Some will go only a short distance. But others will go thousands and thousands of miles—perhaps halfway around the earth. Still others will travel medium distances.

In fact, radio waves very often behave in such a crazy fashion that nobody knows what they will do next. Sometimes a wave will go a hundred miles. Then a few hours later the same kind of wave will go thousands of miles. Some waves will travel farther in the daytime than they will at night. Others will go farther at night than in the day.

The explanation for the crazy behavior of radio waves lies in one of the most fascinating and mysterious things in science—the sun. It is what the sun does that decides where radio waves are going.

The sun actually is the most powerful broadcasting station of all. It sends energy down toward the earth.

Up in the sky—about 60 to 200 miles above the earth—there are several layers of air of different thicknesses. These layers of air are called the *ionosphere*. It is above the stratosphere through which jet planes fly.

When the energy from the sun reaches these layers, it electrifies them. During the daytime the sun is strong, and it can electrify several layers down toward the earth. At night, when the sun has disappeared, not so many of the layers are electrified.

As the position of the sun changes every day and night and from summer to winter, the position of the layers in the sky changes, too. Sometimes they are high, sometimes low.

But now comes the most interesting thing about

these electrified layers. They act like big "electrical" mirrors. They reflect a radio wave as a mirror in your home can reflect the light from a flashlight.

Actually, the radio wave "bounces" off the electrical mirrors as you could bounce a ball off the ceiling of a room. If you throw the ball straight at the ceiling, the ball will come straight back to you. But suppose you go to one end of the room and throw the ball at an angle. The ball will go up to the ceiling at an angle and come down again at the other end of the room like this:

The same thing happens with the radio wave. It goes up into the sky at an angle, hits one of the "mirrors," and bounces off at an angle like this:

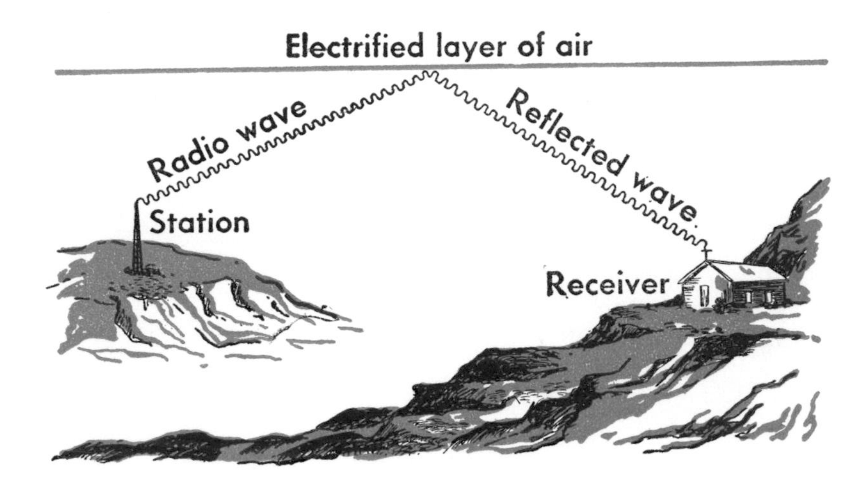


But not every radio wave stops when it comes back to earth. Many waves bounce a second time up toward the sky, hit the electrified layer again, and return to earth still farther away like this:

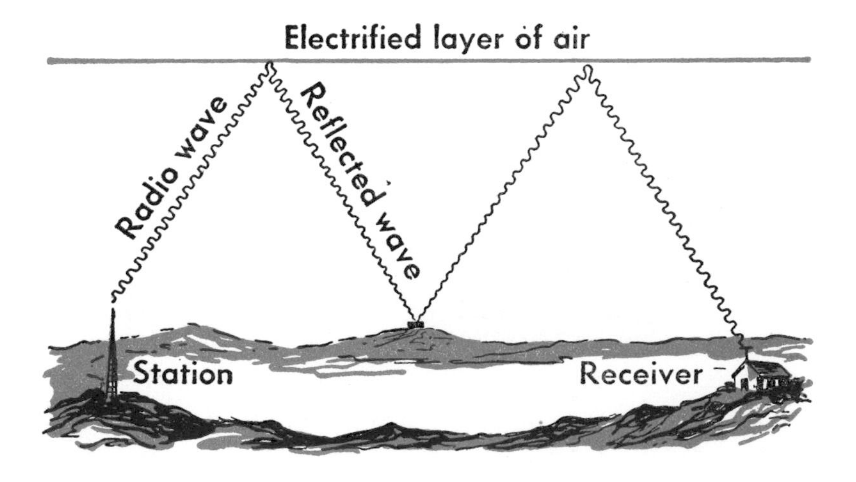

The radio signal can bounce its way across countries and oceans until its energy finally dies out. How far it goes depends on how strong the wave is and how high the electrified layer of air.

Now you can see why the position of the "electrified mirrors" is important. It can determine whether a radio signal skips over a long distance or a short distance.

If the "mirror" is close to the earth, as it is in the daytime, the radio signal can make only short hops like this:

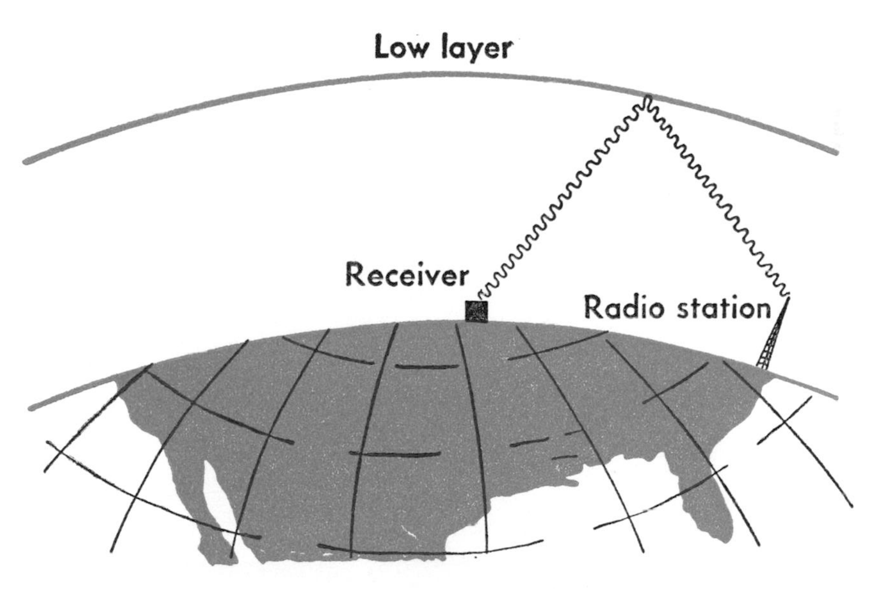


But if the "mirror" is much higher, as it is at night, the signal can make big hops like this:

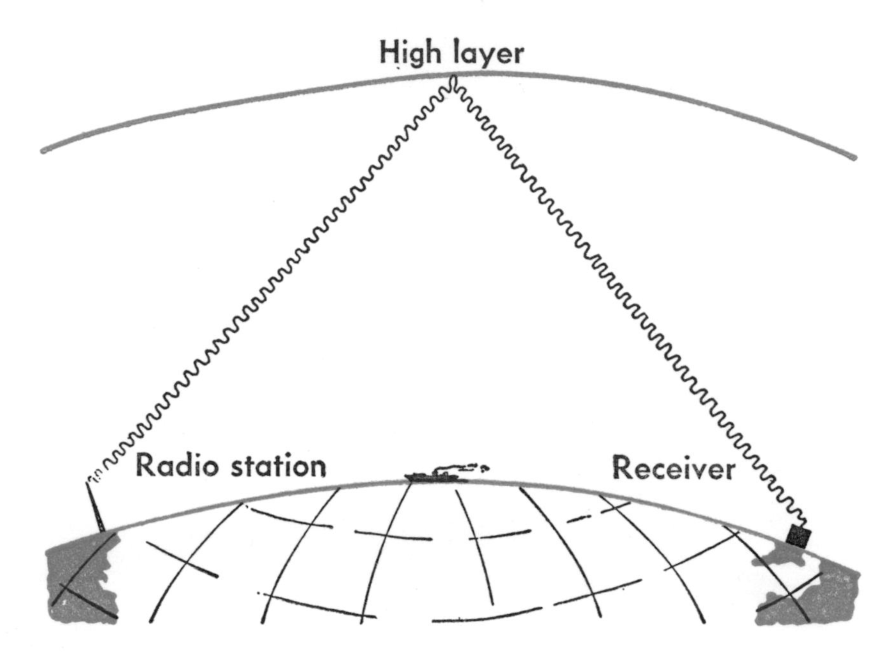


Scientists have discovered another amazing fact about the "mirrors" in the sky. Not all radio waves bounce off the same "mirror." Some radio waves will bounce off a "mirror" low in the sky; other waves will go right through a low "mirror" and will bounce off a higher "mirror."

It is the length of a wave which determines the "mirror" that it uses. The waves that carry programs to a regular radio set use a low "mirror." This means they only travel a few hundred miles before they start losing their strength very rapidly.

Actually, in regular radio not all the waves go up

toward the sky. Some stay close to the ground and for this reason are called "ground waves." They go to your home like this:

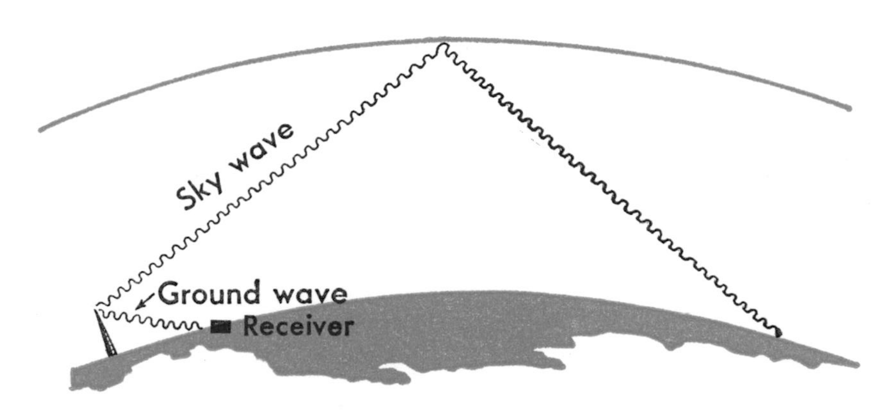


Waves that go along the ground do not travel very far. In fact they travel only about as far as television waves. But since they do not have to depend on mirrors in the sky to be bounced along, they are more reliable during both day and night.

Because ground waves only go a limited distance and sky waves are uncertain, we have the same problem in radio that we have in television. We must connect the stations in a network if we want people all over the country to hear and see the same program clearly. In radio, this is done with telephone wires that spread out to hundreds of towns and cities.

But radio stations using short waves can do many things that a regular station cannot. These short waves go right through the low "mirror" and bounce against a "mirror" higher up like this:

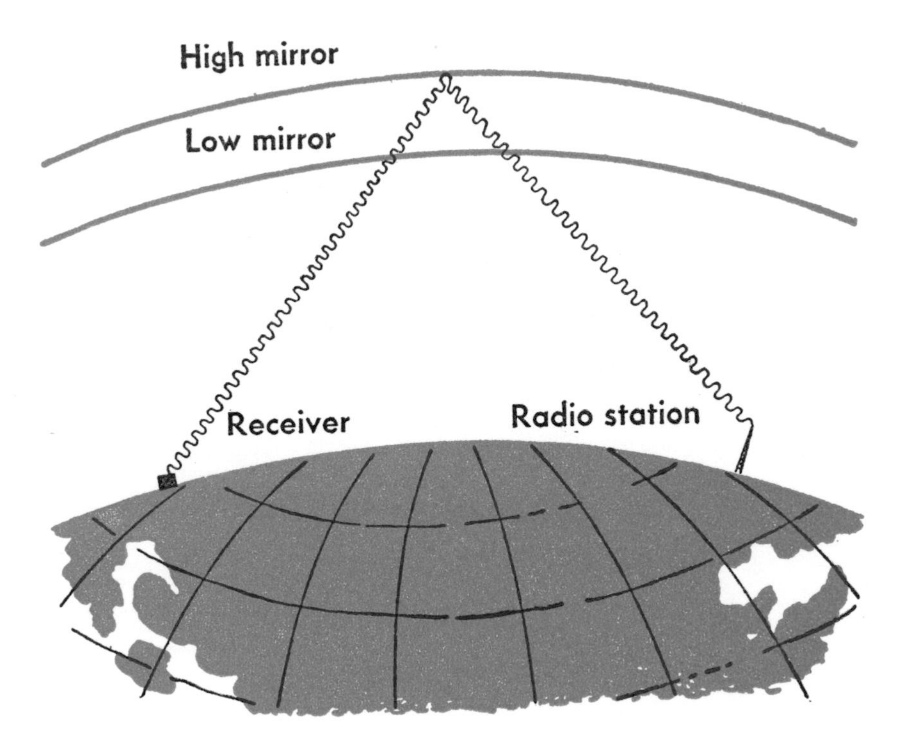


This means that on each hop through the sky short waves will carry a program hundreds and hundreds of miles and, with several hops, thousands of miles. It does not make any difference whether they go across water or land. Short waves do not know anything about boundaries and go from one country to another.

With a short wave radio set, you can hear stations in almost all foreign lands and listen to dozens of different languages.

These international short wave stations have big problems. With the "mirrors" constantly changing their position in the sky, the wave heard at a faraway place may be strong sometimes and weak sometimes. This is called *fading*. Often there are strange spots on the sun which will disturb all the "mirrors" in the sky so that no short wave signals can get through.

A major purpose of the International Geophysical Year in 1957-58 was to learn more about these disturbances. One of the great values of the earth satellites was that they sent signals from outer space down through the ionosphere to earth. This was like looking at the ionosphere from a new direction.

Engineers already have discovered that disturbances in outer space can be extremely useful. Miles above the earth there is a steady stream of "radio clouds," little blobs of wildly active electrons. By aiming powerful transmitters at these clouds, signals can be made to bounce back to earth a thousand miles away, even when other short wave transmissions may be inaudible.

Because this system—it is another form of "scatter propagation"—eliminates the fading caused by shifting "mirrors," it is being used by the Army, Navy and Air Corps.

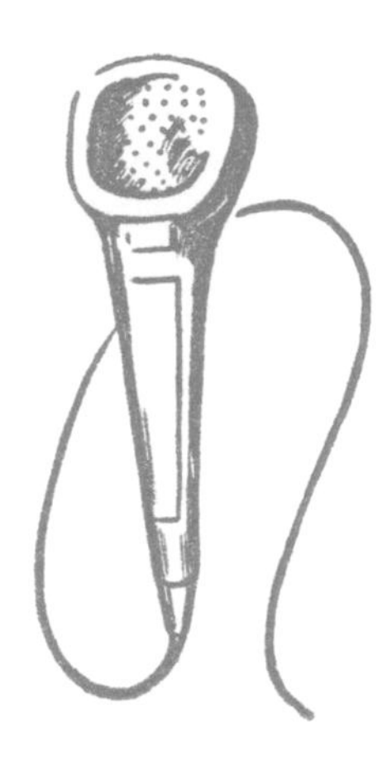

# 15.

# Policeman of the Air

Suppose an enemy spy tried to operate a radio station to send secret messages across the ocean. Or a gangster used a transmitter to outwit detectives.

In a short time both would be caught. There is a "policeman of the air" to see that all kinds of stations obey the law and that the operators of illegal stations are tracked down and sent to jail.

This "policeman" is known as the Federal Communications Commission. The F.C.C. was set up by Congress as an agency of the government.

When radio first started, there was no "policeman." Stations could just go on the air and pick any spot on the dial that they chose. But it was not long before the government realized that something had to be done or radio would be of no use. Stations interfered with each other, and often the listener heard only funny squeals and whistles.

Every radio and television station in the country must secure permission from the F.C.C. before it can go on the air. The F.C.C. issues a license to each station and decides what shall be its place on the dial or whether it shall operate on Channel 2, 4 or 13. In other words, the F.C.C. assigns the frequency on which a station must send out its waves.

No good station wants to get in trouble with the F.C.C. Losing a license means a station must give up the chance to earn thousands or millions of dollars. When each station stays in its own place, many more people can use the air.

But once in a while someone tries to operate a station without a license. To catch stations like this—often they are called "underground" stations—the F.C.C. has its own investigators. They have special tricky ways to find the "outlaws of the air."

Suppose there is an illegal station somewhere in the middle of the United States. Perhaps it is located in an old deserted barn on a lonely road. Twice a day it sends out secret messages in a strange code.

In different parts of the country the F.C.C. has what it calls "monitoring stations." At these places, men listen to their receivers hour after hour. They know all the familiar signals from licensed stations. They are listening particularly for unfamiliar signals which may tell of an illegal station.

Suddenly one of these F.C.C. men hears a new and unfamiliar signal. Immediately all the F.C.C. monitoring centers are alerted. With special equipment each center can tell exactly from which direction the signal is coming.

In Washington a map of the United States is put on a desk. As each F.C.C. monitor reports, a line is drawn to indicate the direction from which that monitor heard the signal. Soon there are several lines, and the map looks like this:

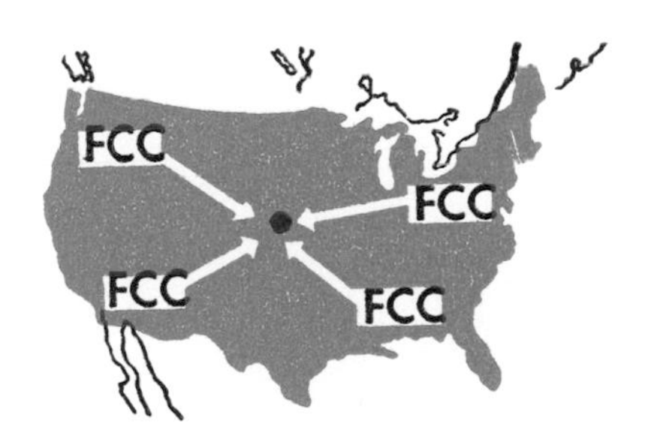

The person operating the illegal station doesn't know it, but he has been found out. Where all the lines cross is the place from which the secret signals are being sent. The F.C.C. is ready to close in.

A special car equipped with receiving equipment is sent to the spot where the lines cross. In the car is a radio compass which shows the direction of the signal. A meter shows whether the signal is getting stronger or weaker.

The car drives in the direction that shows the signal is getting stronger and stronger. Closer and closer it comes to the transmitter. Soon it finds its way to the lonely road. Before long the F.C.C. car is right next to the deserted barn. In a matter of minutes the illegal operator is arrested.

Most countries of the world have their own "radio policemen" and work together so that radio stations in one nation will not interfere with those in another. The different frequencies on which waves are sent out are divided up under international agreement.

But not all nations do co-operate, and this has led to a "war of the air waves." Some countries deliberately try to interfere with programs sent out by other countries. When they do this, we say they *jam* the signals sent out by the other stations. They do it by sending out whistles and spluttery noises on exactly the same frequency as the broadcast. This makes it very difficult and often impossible to hear the stations.

During World War II the practice of "jamming" was used by Germany, but the Nazis found out that it did not always work out as they expected. Several times the Allies made them hopping mad. What the Allies did was to put a station on exactly the same frequency as the German station. Instead of trying to "jam" the Nazi broadcasts, they made fun of them. They did this by waiting until a German speaker had to catch his breath. Then they slipped in their own comment.

What the German listener heard was something like this:

> GERMAN STATION: Hitler is a great man. . . .
>
> ALLIED STATION: Who says so?
>
> GERMAN STATION: And he's a great leader.
>
> ALLIED STATION: Ha, ha, ha!

The Nazis went crazy.

# 16.

# "Calling All Cars"

Most of us think of broadcasting as sending programs out into the air for millions of people to enjoy. That is an important part of broadcasting because it provides entertainment. People always need some entertainment to go along with their work.

But there is another kind of broadcasting which, in some ways, is even more important than entertainment. This is the broadcasting that goes on every day and every night but which most people never see or hear. Some of this is radio; some of this is television.

Often it is easy to forget the real magic—and usefulness—of radio. It is not only that voices can be sent back and forth through the air but that this can be done while both the transmitter and the receiver are moving. You are familiar with a moving receiver because this is what you have when you turn on a radio in a car. As you go speeding along the road, you can listen to music or news reports.

It is just as easy to put a transmitter in a car. You can use the same aerial—the long rod that goes up above the top of the car and looks like a fishing pole. All you need is a button. When you push the button, you can transmit and talk to another car or a central headquarters. Release the button, and you are ready to hear someone speak to you.

When we put a receiver and a transmitter together like this, we have a *radiotelephone*. We can install radiotelephones in cars, ships, airplanes, railroad trains, buses, trucks and taxicabs. Even if you are riding on a lonely road, or high in the sky over a range of mountains, or out in the middle of the ocean, you can always be in touch with the world!

The list of special things that radio and television can do is a long and interesting one. In going down the list, you will be able to see for yourself why broadcasting can be so fascinating.

## Police Radio Car

Police departments all over the country have used radio for many years because it is often the quickest way to catch criminals.

Suppose someone telephones the police to say that his house is being robbed. This is what happens:

The sergeant answering the telephone in the police station asks for the address of the house where the robbery is taking place. He passes the information on to the radio dispatcher, who knows where the radio patrol cars are cruising around the city.

He notifies the cars nearest to the robbery like this: "Calling Cars 12 and 14!"

The dispatcher tells the policemen in the cars the address of the crime and then adds "Signal 35." The policemen know that "Signal 35" means a robbery. Other signals may mean a man has a gun, or there is

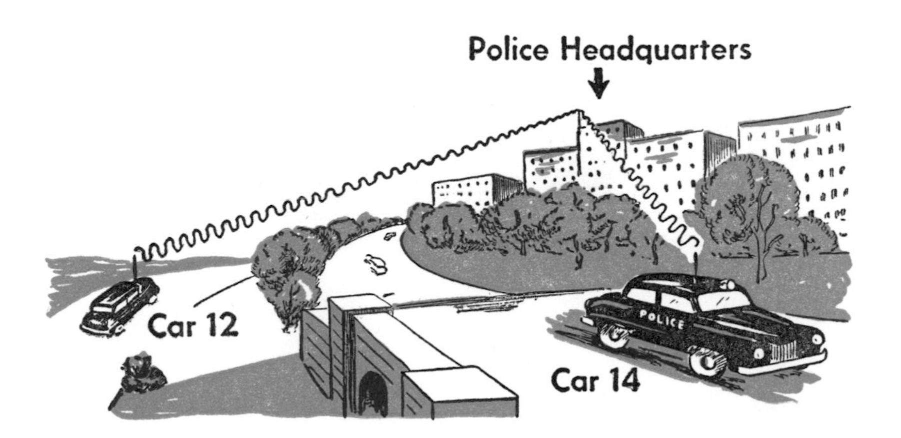


an automobile accident, or someone is just disturbing the peace of the community. Different police departments have different signals.

In a matter of minutes after receiving the alarm, the radio patrol cars are at the scene of the crime. Often they catch a robber before he even has a chance to get out of a house. In the days before radio, the police would have to send a car all the way from headquarters, which might have been many miles away. Often they arrived too late.

#### Amateur Radio

A great hobby for many people in many countries is called *amateur radio.* The amateur radio operator has his own radio station on which he can talk or send out messages in code. Then when he is finished, another operator answers him.

With no more power than it takes to light a 60 watt bulb, an amateur in the United States can communicate by short wave with another amateur in Europe or South America. The amateurs call themselves "*hams*" for short.

Before you can have your own short wave station, you must obtain a license. The American Radio Relay League, national association of amateur radio operators, publishes a series of booklets explaining exactly how to become an amateur and have your own station. A postcard to the League's headquarters in West Hartford, Connecticut, will bring you all the information.

### Radio on a Train

The newest railroad trains use radio in many different ways. In the club car where passengers can smoke or order refreshments, there is a radiotelephone in a booth, just like the telephone booth in a drugstore. All the passenger does is lift the receiver in the booth and ask for the operator. Then the passenger can call any number in the country.

Another use for radio is on freight trains. The engineer in the locomotive has a radiotelephone which he uses to call the brakeman in the caboose like this:

If a freight train has a hundred cars, you can see how much easier it is to use radio than to walk on top of the cars all the way up to the engineer. Or if the engineer wants, he can talk to the engineer of a train coming in the opposite direction.

## Radio at Sea

Big ocean-going ships have many kinds of radio, too. One radio is tuned always to what is known as *the international distress frequency*. This is the frequency which can be used by a ship only when it is in danger of sinking or needs help immediately. It is the S O S frequency.

Ships also have radiotelephones for the passengers which are called *ship-to-shore* telephones. Then, there are short wave radios to pick up the news and weather reports.

### Radio in the Air

Airplanes depend on radio for their take-off, their flight and their landing. The pilot has several different radiotelephones in a big plane because sometimes he must use different wave lengths, depending on whether he wants to send a message over a long distance or a short distance.

When a plane goes out on the runway, the control tower at the airport uses radio to tell the pilot when he is to take off. Once the plane is in the air, the pilot is told at what altitude he must fly. Except in an emergency, when he does whatever he thinks best, a pilot cannot change his altitude without obtaining permission from the nearest control tower.

There is another protection for airplanes flying through the air. It is called *riding the beam*. The *beam* is really just a continuous series of radio signals sent out in one direction in the same way that a flashlight will send out a beam of light. It looks like this:

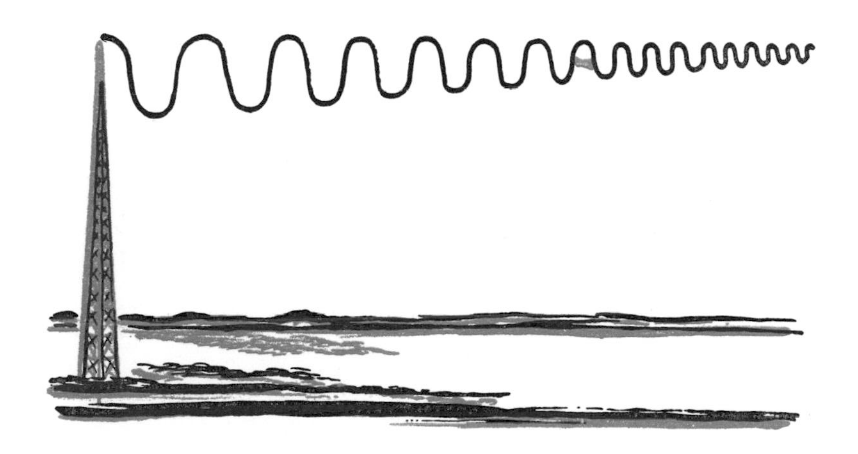

As long as the pilot hears the signals, he knows he is "on the beam" and will be guided straight to his destination.

At the landing field, another control tower uses radio to tell the pilot if it is his turn to land, or whether he must circle around overhead—the pilots call this being "stacked up"—until the runways are clear.

### Walkie-Talkie

The *walkie-talkie* used by soldiers is really just a small radiotelephone. It is intended for use only over short distances, a few miles at most, so not very many tubes are needed and the equipment is light enough for one man to carry. Walkie-talkies are often used by firemen at big fires. Often it is important for a fireman to be able to call the fire truck and order more hose or equipment.

**Underwater Television**

Television still is so new that scientists constantly are discovering new ways to use the camera. Recently, the English Navy found it helpful in locating a submarine that had sunk. They put a television camera in a watertight container and then dropped it over the side of a rescue ship. When they turned the camera on, they were able to see the submarine in deep water like this:

Perhaps some day television can be used to find the wrecks of ancient pirate ships or to explore other mysteries at the bottom of the sea.

# 17

# Round-Trip to the Moon

Ever since the beginning of time, man always has wished that he could see in darkness. Now he can through an invention that already has changed the course of history. It is the invention of *radar*.

The word radar stands for *Radio Detection and Ranging*. "Detection" means to find out where something is, and "ranging" means to find out how far away that something is and, if it is moving, where it is going.

That is what radar does. It uses waves to go out into space and bring back a picture of what lies farther away than the eye can see. Darkness, fog, storm and smoke screens do not affect these waves. The electronic "eyes" of radar are ready always to warn us of trouble ahead.

It was radar that helped save England from the German airplanes during World War II. The Nazis sent swarms of planes over London in what is called "The Battle of Britain." They hoped to crush the capital of the British Empire, which was then fighting almost alone, and to end the war quickly. England had only a few airplanes but very brave pilots.

With the help of radar, English airmen knew when Nazi planes were coming long before they reached London. With their few airplanes, they took off quickly and were in the sky when the Nazis arrived. Instead of finding London a defenseless city, the Nazis found the British ready for dogfights. After several raids, the Germans lost so many airplanes that the Nazi air force was never the same again. It was one of the turning points of the war.

Radar works like a rubber ball thrown against a stone wall.

If we throw a ball fast enough against a wall, we know that it will come right back to us like this:

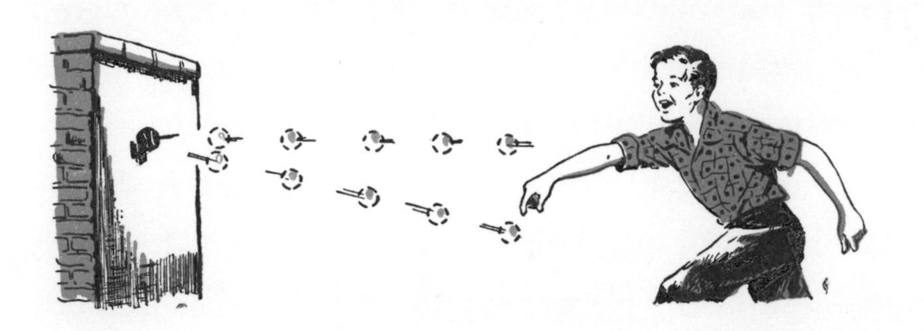

Now imagine that we knew how fast we threw the ball. Suppose we say that in one second the ball traveled ten feet.

Let's throw the ball against the wall a second time and have a friend hold a watch and tell us how long it takes the ball to make the round trip from your hand, up to the wall and back again to your hand.

Our friend looks at his watch and says the round trip took exactly two seconds. Now we can show what happened like this:

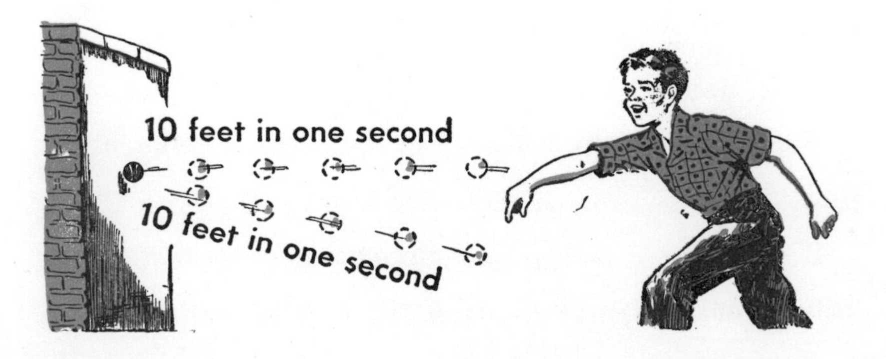

We know that in each second the ball can travel ten feet.

Since it took two seconds for the round trip, that means the ball traveled a total of twenty feet.

But we only want to know how far away the wall is from your hand. So we divide the round trip in half. Half of twenty is ten. So the distance from the hand to the wall is ten feet.

In radar, it is the wave that takes the place of the rubber ball. At a radar station, a transmitter and a receiver are put side by side.

First, a signal—called a *pulse*—makes a wave that is sent out into the air from the transmitter. Then the transmitter is shut off, and the receiver is turned on. The signal goes out until it "hits" something like the stone wall—maybe it is a ship or maybe it is a plane. Then the signal bounces off the ship or the plane and comes back to the receiver. When it gets to the receiver, the signal goes to a picture tube and makes a tiny flicker of light.

We know a radio signal always travels at the same speed—186,000 miles a second. And we easily can tell how long the signal traveled. We measure the time between when it left the transmitter and when it came back to the receiver. So now we can tell how far the signal traveled. Just as we did with the rubber ball, we then divide that distance in half and we know how far away the plane is. We can show it like this:

With a real radar set all the calculations are done automatically. All the radar operator does is look at the picture tube, and he gets his answer right away.

Because radio signals travel so much faster than the airplane, radar can follow the plane right across the sky. The face of the radar screen is divided into little squares. Then, on the screen, it shows where the plane is going to be in a couple of seconds like this:

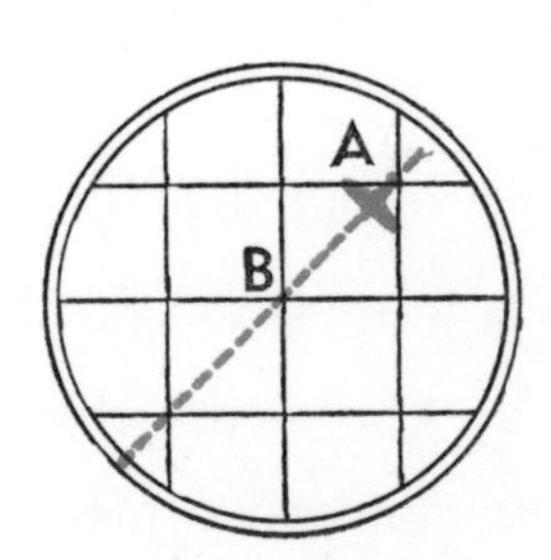

If the plane is first spotted at A, we know it will soon be at B.

This is time enough to aim and fire a shell from a gun if the plane is sent over by an enemy. The shell arrives at B just at the same moment as the plane. Down goes the plane in an explosion!

Another kind of radar sends out and receives a lot of waves. When enough waves are bounced back, it gives us a whole picture of what they have "hit," like this:

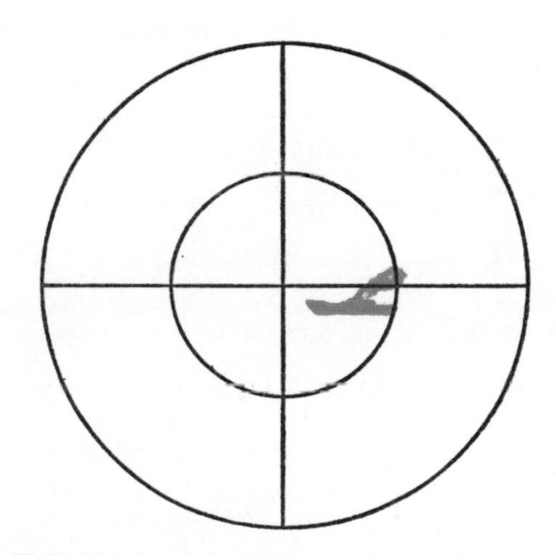

You can see how important radar is to ships and airplanes that must go through darkness, storms and fogs. One ship can tell if another ship is crossing its path, or if there is an iceberg ahead. Radar is so sensitive that it can even pick out the conning tower of an enemy submarine.

With radar, an airplane can tell if there is a mountain ahead, or if it is flying too close to the ground. Small radar sets are put in bombers and jet planes. With radar, although the bombardier often cannot see the target with his eye, he can put the bomb right where he wants it.

But the most dramatic story of radar took place on a lonely hill in New Jersey on a cold night in January, 1946. On the hill was a plain wooden building surrounded by high fences. Soldiers were on guard.

On top of the building was a strange rectangular piece of metal. It looked like a big bedspring, and it was pointed up to the heavens. It was a special radar aerial.

Inside the building, there were Army officers huddled over mysterious looking radar sets. Everyone was very still. Hour after hour they waited. An officer finally looked at his watch. "All right," he said.

Suddenly there was heard in the room a signal that sounded like this:

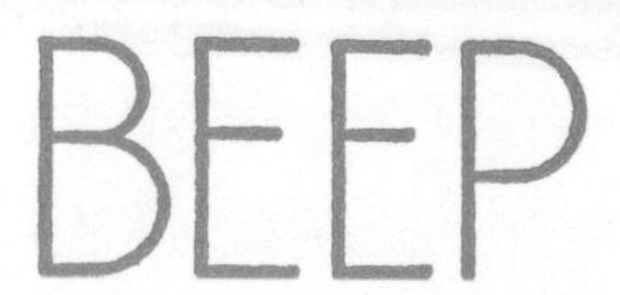

Everyone held his breath and counted to himself:

One

Two

They waited a fraction of a second more. Then they heard the sound that was to make history:

*BEEP*

For the first time, man had shown that he could "communicate" with the moon!

The big "beep" was a radar signal sent up to the face of the moon. The little *beep* was all the strength that the signal had left, after it had come back to earth like this:

Twelve years later—in 1957—there were the more famous "beeps" heard around the world—the signals transmitted from Sputnik I, the first man-made earth satellite.

The inside of a satellite is crammed with electronic equipment. One nation can send up a satellite and it will pick up information about winds, temperatures and pressures in all parts of the world; the satellite can relay this information to earth each time it passes its starting point. Some day there will be cameras in the nose of space ships. Pictures of how the world looks from the outside will be transmitted to ground. And millions of people will be able to see what lies in outer space.

Only sixty years ago—less than the average lifetime of a person—radio and television were only dreams.

# Index

# Index

# Index

# Index